Revealing Antiquity

· 12 ·

G. W. Bowersock, General Editor

KINSHIP DIPLOMACY
IN THE
ANCIENT
WORLD

Christopher P. Jones

HARVARD UNIVERSITY PRESS
CAMBRIDGE, MASSACHUSETTS
LONDON, ENGLAND
1999

Library of Congress Cataloging-in-Publication Data

Jones. C. P. (Christopher Prestige), 1940–
Kinship diplomacy in the ancient world / Christopher P. Jones
p.   cm. — (Revealing antiquity : 12)
Includes bibliographical references and index.
ISBN 0-674-50527-1 (alk. paper)
1. Kinship—Greece—History. 2. Kinship—Rome—History.
3. Greece—Foreign relations. 4. Rome—Foreign relations.
5. Civilization, Greco-Roman. I. Title. II. Series.
GN585.G85J66   1999
306.83'09495—dc21
98-44084

ACKNOWLEDGMENTS

I am grateful to the several audiences to which I have presented some of the ideas and material in this book—at Harvard and the Universities of Bordeaux, Cincinnati, and Toronto; at the Ecole Normale Supérieure, Paris, where I gave a series of seminars in May 1992; and to those Harvard students who participated in a seminar in the fall term of the same year. I have also to thank Kevin Daly and Alex Inglis for assistance given in many ways.

More recently, four friends read a draft of this book and helped me greatly by their comments—Glen Bowersock, Christian Habicht, Simon Hornblower, and Gregory Nagy. I have also profited from the comments of the two readers for Harvard University Press. Other debts are acknowledged in their place.

I also owe thanks to the people and institutions who supplied the illustrations and gave permission to reproduce them: to the Trustees of the British Museum for Figures 1, 3, and 5; to the American Numismatic Society for Figure 2; and to Professor R. R. R. Smith, Project Director of the New York University excavations at Aphrodisias, Caria, for Figure 4.

CONTENTS

ILLUSTRATIONS

KINSHIP DIPLOMACY
IN THE ANCIENT WORLD

INTRODUCTION

In every stage of these Oppressions We have Petitioned for Redress in the most humble terms . . . Nor have we been wanting in attentions to our British brethren. We have warned them from time to time of attempts by their legislature to extend an unwarrantable jurisdiction over us. We have reminded them of the circumstances of our emigration and settlement here. We have appealed to their native justice and magnanimity, and we have conjured them by the ties of our common kindred to disavow these usurpations, which would inevitably interrupt our connections and correspondence. They too have been deaf to the voice of justice and of consanguinity. We must, therefore, acquiesce in the necessity, which denounces our Separation, and hold them, as we hold the rest of mankind, Enemies in War, in Peace Friends.

Among its other purposes, The Declaration of Independence justified the American Revolution to the people of the thirteen states no less than to the world at large. When Thomas Jefferson wrote the paragraph above, consciously or unconsciously he was echoing the language of Greek and Roman diplomacy, in which kinship was frequently invoked. The language of kinship, the appeal to "brothers" or "the family of civilized nations," continues in use today.

For the founding fathers, words such as "brethren" and "consanguinity" were not terms of diplomacy so much as rhetorical devices to emphasize the misconduct of the British government toward a people whose roots were largely in the British Isles. In the diplomacy of the ancient world, appeals to brotherhood and kinship had a far more concrete meaning. They referred occasionally to colonization in the recorded past, but more often to kinship created by direct descent from specific persons, either gods or heroes, in an epoch almost before history. Such appeals are found from the earliest time for which we have significant evidence about Greek diplomacy—the period of the Persian Wars—well into the late Roman empire. The high point is the period of roughly three hundred years following the death of Alexander of Macedon, the "Hellenistic" era which in some ways is the Middle Ages of Greco-Roman antiquity.

The following chapters trace this "kinship diplomacy" through its recorded history in the Greco-Roman world and assess it as a factor in international relations. Why did the Greeks, who will be the main actors, use this device so frequently? On what sort of occasion did they use it? If it was a "propaganda ploy," how effective was it? What does it tell us about the Greeks' conception of themselves, and about other peoples' conceptions of them?

Asking these questions will lead us to consider others, such as the role of religion in ancient diplomacy. In marked contrast to modern western diplomacy, which is highly secular, Greek diplomats not only were regarded as under the special protection of the gods, but also performed religious rites in the host city. Hence their appeals invoked the gods and heroes who were common to their home city and to the city to which they had been sent. By a natural extension, again in stark contrast to modern diplomacy, diplomats could cite literary sources to advance their claims, not only historians but also poets, and some ambassadors even gave musical recitals of the texts. Thus arises a related question which has been much debated, whether the Greeks believed in their myths. The *prima facie* answer which such transactions suggest is that they did.

Another question that will arise concerns the self-perception of the Greeks, and by extension of the Romans. Nineteenth-century scholarship is sometimes accused of glorifying northern invaders such as the Dorians and concealing the debt which the Greeks themselves acknowledged to Semitic and African peoples. We shall see that the web of Greek diplomacy really was centered on Greek gods and heroes, and that claims of kinship with Semitic peoples are unusual, while claims of kinship with African peoples, including the Egyptians, are virtually nonexistent.

Throughout this book I have assumed that kinship diplomacy is a historical phenomenon in the truest sense, that is, something that can be perceived across a variety of instances and subjected to explanation. On that assumption, I have attempted a sequential narrative of this phenomenon as it emerges at the beginning of Greek literature and ends in a world that is both Greek and Roman, that of early Byzantium. Such a procedure might be labeled "positivist" insofar as it assumes "a real objective past that is external to the historical analyst."[1] Yet the object of the search is something not strictly "objective," but "subjective" at least to the actors, a way of thinking about their past and of behaving in their present. If the comparison does not seem overly fanciful, kinship diplomacy is like a rainbow, something which may be observed in certain meteorological conditions and from a limited range of viewpoints, an objective reality and at the same time an optical illusion. This book sets out, not to grasp that rainbow, but to trace its arc in the specific context of Greco-Roman antiquity.

This book is not a study either of ethnic identity or of "fictive kinship." The subject of ethnic identity has been treated very well by others and requires a mastery of disciplines to which I lay no claim.[2] I have avoided the term "fictive kinship" partly because diplomatic kinship was usually not, so far as can be judged, a fiction to the actors. Though they can sometimes be convicted of using proofs which modern analysis inclines to judge spurious, there are almost no instances in which they can be shown to have done so deliberately and consciously. Nor is such kinship fictive in the sense of being called into existence by law, custom, or ritual, as (for example) adoptive relationships are often described in Greek as existing "by act" *(thesei)* as opposed to "by nature" *(physei)*.

Accordingly it also follows that this book is not about myth.[3] Though I have used the word "mythical" to indicate that a relationship is based on figures whom we would consider fabulous or legendary, such as Heracles, Perseus, or Jason, the actors tend not to use the term "myth," probably because of its connotation of falsity or fable. It has often been observed that myth is the ancient history of the Greeks, and is separated from what we would call history only by the degree of uncertainty and often contradictoriness that surrounds "mythic" traditions. Moreover, though diplomats tend to appeal more often to links that we would call mythic than to historical ones, that is because such links have the sanction of antiquity, of "gods and heroes." Similar links could also be created in historical time, for example by recent colonization. Thus the great collection of documents referring to the "cousins" of Magnesia on the Maeander involves both migrations in the time of the heroes and the colonizing activities of the Seleucids.[4]

It is customary to regard the diplomatic use of kinship as a phenomenon of the Hellenistic period, and certainly huge collections of documents such as those from Magnesia encourage such a view. But it will emerge that diplomatic pleas of a similar kind are attested since at least the early fifth century, and not only between Greek states but in the intercourse of Greeks with non-Greeks, for example with the Persian empire. Well before Rome entered the theater of the eastern Mediterranean in the late third century, it too had become a node in the huge network of diplomatic relations and mythical kinships, and its growing domination did nothing to arrest this commerce of religion and myth. Indeed it encouraged it, and the emperor Hadrian's involvement in the Panhellenion, a federation of Greek cities from the eastern empire, was merely the reification of the same tradition. As late as Justinian I, Byzantine emperors continued to be amenable to pleas of kinship between states. What caused kinship diplomacy to die out was in part the lessening importance of the Greek city as a unit within the Roman empire. No less important was the emergence of a religion which did not acknowledge the living force of pagan gods and heroes, but saw the kinship between human and divine in new terms all its own.

I

THE LANGUAGE OF

KINSHIP DIPLOMACY

*N*ear the farthest point of his conquests, in what is now southern Pakistan, Alexander the Great encountered a tribe called the Siboi, a wild people dressed in skins and carrying clubs. To the Greek mind, their appearance could only recall the prince of heroes, Heracles, and later historians, perhaps relying on reports from Alexander's staff, identified the Siboi as descendants of Heracles and his companions. By a coincidence, the royal house of Macedon traced its origin to Temenus, a descendant of Heracles from Argos in the Peloponnese. From this time on, the legend of an Indian campaign was added to the list of Heracles' exploits.[1]

The meeting between Alexander and his Indian kinsmen is narrated by several extant writers, of whom one is the Sicilian historian Diodorus, writing at the end of the Hellenistic period. Like other Hellenistic historians, Diodorus was strongly interested in the legendary past of Greece and its continuation into historical time, and for him this incident derived special piquancy from its conjunction of myth and history. He therefore gives a detailed account of the king's encounter with the Siboi. Unlike the other sources, he says nothing about their savage appearance, but describes them as inhabiting a "very distinguished city" *(polis)*. When Alexander pitched his camp nearby, "the citizens first in reputation approached and, being received in audience by the king and renewing [*ananeōsamenoi*] their kinship, promised to act in every way as his kinsmen [*syngeneis*], and brought him magnificent gifts. Accepting [*apodechomenos*] their goodwill, the king declared their cities free, and proceeded against the neighboring tribes."[2]

Diodorus thus turns the story of Alexander's meeting with the Siboi into a type of diplomatic exchange particularly common in the Hellenistic period. The city selects its most influential citizens to lead a deputation to the higher power; the ambassadors are received in audience; they proceed to "recall" the "kinship" between the king and their own community; he "approves" the city's gesture and reciprocates with his own act of goodwill, in this case by declaring it free and proceeding onward.

How much historical truth lies behind this account is now unrecoverable. It is certain, however, that every item of the language used by Diodorus corresponds with actual practice. "Renewal" of inherited links implies not merely calling them to mind, but establishing them to the satisfaction of the party to whom the delegation is addressed.[3] Very often, as here, it is part of a process of supplication, which is so central to ancient diplomacy that the Greek term for embassy *(presbeia)* comes eventually to mean "prayer of intercession." Similarly, "acceptance" designates the decision of the stronger, or advantaged, party to act in accordance with the arguments of the weaker one, and by the time of Diodorus had long since acquired the sense of "approval." The crucial term is "kinsmen" *(syngeneis)*. Since Heracles and his companions had left progeny behind who were the ancestors of the present Siboi, these were related, however distantly, to the Macedonian king who now made his appearance outside their city, and could turn the relationship to their own advantage.

In its original form the story goes back to historians contemporary with Alexander, who wished to display his magnanimity, and perhaps to disguise what might have seemed a military failure as an act of piety toward his heroic ancestor. Whoever the original source was, however, neither he nor Diodorus seems to have doubted that the king's action was both credible and creditable. The story thus raises larger questions of the relationship between myth, in this case a myth of Heracles' wanderings, and history. Even if it is itself a myth, insofar as it is an invention of historical apologists, still it implies an acceptance on Alexander's part of his own descent from a mythic hero and of his duty to act properly by his Indian kinsmen, in other words a recognition of both a vertical relationship and a horizontal one.

The nature and status of ancient myth, and its relation to history, have been much discussed, and for the present purpose it will perhaps be enough to observe some generalities, with a particular emphasis on the Greeks. (Though the Romans play no less important a role in this narration, for most of the concepts and terms that matter here they are dependent on Greek thought.) It is true that Greek historiography began with the attempt to eliminate the fabulous and the supernatural from accounts of the past, and early practitioners like Herodotus criticized inventions of poets, whose very name meant "makers." Later historians are more tolerant. The fourth-century Ephorus, the first to attempt a history of all times and places, began not with "ancient mythology" but with the "return of the Heraclidae," the campaigns of Heracles' descendants to regain their rightful possessions in the Peloponnese.[4] His decision reflects a fundamental distinction between layers of myth. Unlike those concerned with the creation of the world and the early lives and adventures of the gods, those which narrate the actions of heroes, beings halfway between human and divine, represented the beginnings of the knowable past. "The Greeks were persuaded," it has been said, "that the heroic mythology was their ancient history."[5]

On this point the two classic historians of Greece, Herodotus and Thucydides, so different in so many ways, are in agreement. Herodotus separates the very earliest history from what he calls "the so-called human generation" *(hē legomenē anthrōpēiē geneē),* when gods and heroes walked the earth and mingled with mortals; in this case he is talking of Minos, the legendary king of Crete, whose reign was still a palpable entity for Greeks of the fifth century, as it has become again with the discoveries of Sir Arthur Evans. Herodotus' opening chapters, tracing the Persian Wars to a feud between Greeks and barbarians that began with the wanderings of the Argive heroine Io, represent the same kind of thought. When he comes down to events near his own time, however, he does not admit gods or heroes as direct agents into his tale. They may intervene invisibly, as when the wrath of the legendary hero Talthybius falls on the Spartans for having killed Persian ambassadors. By contrast, when describing the alleged encounter of the runner Pheidippides with the god Pan, Herodotus tells the story in such a way as to withhold his own authority. In the two places where he uses the word "myth," it is to derogate the inventions of Homer and other storytellers.[6]

Thucydides too rejects "the mythic" as an ingredient of historiography, but though his target is Herodotus, he refers to his predecessor's taste for diverting stories such as that of Candaules' wife.[7] He too regards the heroic age as part of history, and again Minos serves as the exemplar, being "the most ancient of those whom we know by tradition [*akoē,* literally "hearing"] to have built a navy." His digression on the ancestry of the Thracian king Sitalces shows that, like Herodotus, he rejected the embroidery with which poets had embellished Greek myth, but not the historicity of myth itself.[8]

Thus Alexander of Macedon could easily believe that the gods were not merely beings enthroned in heaven, but had once walked the earth and left mortal progeny, of which he was one. A barbarous people in the mountains of Afghanistan could therefore be his kinsmen, "of joint descent" *(syngeneis)*. The first term of this compound denotes association or community. The second, *genos,* comes from an Indo-European root denoting birth, and similar formations exist in other languages, for example *genus* in Latin. In the *Iliad,* the primary meaning of *genos* is "birth" in the sense of origin. An individual, whether god or human, shares *genos* with another if they have the same father, as for example Hera reminds Zeus that "I too am a god, and my *genos* is from the same source as yours." Less often, *genos* also has the sense of "race" or "kind," for example "the race of half-divine men" *(hēmitheōn genos andrōn)*. By a different extension, perhaps occurring only in more recent parts of the poem, the word can also refer to the whole line of a person's ancestors, as when Glaucus the Lycian is told by his father "not to disgrace the line [*genos*] of my fathers, who were born [*egenonto*] of highest birth in Ephyre and in broad Lycia."[9]

In the archaic era of Greece, the age of the Homeric poems' first audiences, a sense close to the last of those above comes to the fore, *genos* as "clan" or "house."[11] The most prestigious of such "descent-groups," to use the anthropological term, trace their lineage from a common ancestor, always male and sometimes a "hero," that is, a semidivine being who is either the son or a remoter descendant of a god or goddess. His name, with the addition of the patronymic suffix *−idēs* or *−adēs,* is used in the plural for all the members. These clans played different roles in different communities, sometimes claiming hereditary access to certain prized skills or roles. Thus at Sparta the Talthybiadae descended from Talthybius, the herald of Agamemnon, and had the exclusive right to act as public messengers. In some communities such clans supplied the royal family, as for example the rulers of Macedon were "Temenidae" because of their descent from the "Heraclid" Temenus.[11]

As the Greeks began to reflect on their origins and their differences, both among themselves and between themselves and their neighbors, it was natural to explain cultural markers such as language and customs by invoking common descent, and to use the term *genos* for groups marked by shared attributes. It was also natural to suppose that such races, like the family groups which constituted them, went back to a single significant ancestor, and the now fragmentary poem attributed to Hesiod, the *Catalogue of Women,* represents the origin of all the major Greek *genē* by a complex scheme of genealogies.

For the first extant historians, however, this scheme was not satisfactory. Herodotus regards eponyms like Dorus and Ion merely as significant rulers in the history of their respective *genos,* and *genē* as capable of growth by accretion and conquest, not merely by descent. So also for Thucydides, Hellen is a son of Deucalion (the Greek Noah), but his name was transmitted to the Hellenes as he and his sons extended their protection to alien cities.[12] By contrast, in Euripides' *Ion* the hero is not merely the eponym of all Ionians but also their ancestor, though Euripides seems to suppose that the Ionians took his name only in later generations. So also Dorus and Achaeus, the half-brothers of Ion, are both ancestors and eponyms of the Dorians and the Achaeans.[13] Euripides' view seems closer to traditional Greek belief than the speculations of historians, and certainly later texts take it for granted that all free members of a community descend from the legendary founder, as the Siboi descend from Heracles and his companions. The fact that diplomatic appeals based on national "kinship" often fail to specify a single common ancestor, at least before the third century, is probably not to be attributed to a basic change in thinking about such kinships, but rather to the fact that our documents are almost always very brief summaries, and rarely give the full argumentation of the parties involved.[14]

For the propagation of such ancestors across, and often beyond, the boundaries of the Greek world, it was an essential feature of certain of the most notable heroes that they were remembered as wanderers. In extant literature the clearest example is Homer's portrait of Odysseus, but though Odysseus is one such "wandering hero," others were to be much more important in the propagation of "community of descent." Above all, this role suited Heracles, the son of Zeus and a mortal mother, enshrined in myth both for his many travels and for his sexual potency. Moreover, his early fame as a slayer of monsters in time turned him into a champion of human habitation, of civilized and especially Greek life against the untamed forces of nature and barbarity. Sometimes Heracles, like other heroes, was represented as commanding a horde of followers, who after aiding some beleaguered people, or after the death of their leader, settled in a foreign land.[15]

Another such "wandering hero" is Perseus, whose travels began in the womb when his mother, Danaë, became pregnant by Zeus and was banished from Argos. His best-known exploit, the quest for the head of the Gorgon Medusa, was placed either in inner Asia or in Africa, and he too was credited with leaving progeny in the regions he had visited. A well-attested tradition held that the Persians were a *genos* descended from Perses, a son of Perseus. According to a story reported by Herodotus, Xerxes tried to exploit this claim in order to induce his "ancestors," the Argives, to stay neutral in the war with Greece. The belief that such heroes were also the ultimate ancestors of cities or nations was widespread in Greek thought, and was then taken up by the Romans, who call themselves "Aeneadae" as descendants of Aeneas. So also Jewish tradition held that Noah's sons were the ancestors of all the nations of the earth, and that Abraham was the patriarch of all Jews and their near relatives.[16]

A term used for such founding fathers is *archēgetēs,* which signifies "first leader" or "chief leader." It is used by Pindar to designate the hero Tlepolemus as the leader of Dorian settlers from the Peloponnese to Rhodes, and in a document which may go back to the foundation of the Dorian colony of Thera it is applied to Battus, who led a subsidiary group of colonists from Thera to Cyrene in north Africa. The same term is also applied to gods who provided the initial impulse for the foundation, particularly to Apollo, whose oracle at Delphi had to be consulted when a city planned to send out colonists.[17]

Colonization provided another model whereby the Greeks explained the spread of descent-groups *(genē)* across the world. The word "colony" reflects Roman rather than Greek practice and is less expressive than the Greeks' own term, *apoikia,* "away-household." This, like the old American word "out-settlement," emphasizes that Greek colonization involved the division of households between the "mother city" *(mētropolis)* and the "away-household," with a consequent sharing of traditions and obligations between the two. The settlements of the Bronze and early Iron Ages, for example the establishment of Mycenaean traders in such places as Miletus or Tarentum, already constitute a form of colonization, and are sometimes reflected in the myths of classical Greece. But this practice is especially marked in the archaic period, which runs approximately from 800 to 500. This period saw the settlement of Greeks in the western Mediterranean as far as Spain, in the eastern Mediterranean as far as the coast of Syria, from the Crimea in the north to Egypt and Cyrene in the south; and these settlements created bonds which were later to play a powerful role. One example is the ties between Corinth, its colony of Corcyra, and Corcyra's own colony of Epidamnus at the entrance to the Adriatic, whose rupture in the 430s led to the Peloponnesian War.[18] Another such wave of colonization, set in motion by Alexander and continued by the rulers of the successor states, occurred in the early Hellenistic period.[19]

In Greek colonization, even that conducted by Hellenistic rulers, an essential unit was the "city," or *polis*. This term originally meant "citadel," and in Athens as late as the fourth century it was used for the rocky platform later called the Acropolis.[20] For the Dorians an upland area of central Greece, in the region of Mount Parnassus, was their "mother citadel" *(mētropolis),* since it was there, according to legend, that the Heraclidae had begun their long march into the Peloponnese.[21]

In the archaic age, the word *polis* acquired its classic sense of an urban community possessing political organization and certain indispensable structures such as a meeting-place *(agora)*. Aristotle, however, the founder of political science, saw the household *(oikia)* and the house *(oikos)* as the essential and original units of the city.[22] It was the world of the family, not of the city, that engendered many of the terms later essential to kinship diplomacy. The most frequent of these, "community of descent" *(syngeneia),* is not attested in diplomatic discourse until Thucydides. In the previous generation, Herodotus uses a different language, applying terms of vertical relationship even between coevals, so that the Persians, for example, are "descendants" *(apogonoi)* of the contemporary Argives. Thucydides is also the first author to employ the term *mētropolis* to a community which despatches colonies abroad.[23] Later diplomacy uses language such as "sisters" *(adelphai)* for two colonies sharing a single mother city, with "kinsmen" *(syngeneis)* reserved for more distant relationships.

A term which appears frequently in diplomacy is directly derived from *oikos,* but its precise sense is elusive—*oikeios*.[24] Herodotus uses it only of blood relatives, as he does *syngenēs,* though with a different nuance of closeness or nearness.[25] In later Greek it develops a sense of "familiar" or "dear," and the abstract noun *oikeiotēs* can be used of an affective state comparable to friendship *(philia)* or love *(erōs)*.[26] Exactly what sense it has when employed in diplomatic contexts has been disputed, whether it denotes a sort of kinship less close than one implied by *syngeneia,* or rather an affective condition that may exist between states which may or may not be "akin." The latter is certainly its principal sense in the period of imperial Rome, and arguably so even in the classical era.

An influential story told by Herodotus exemplifies the imaginative projection of colonization into the world of myth. The Lydian people of western Asia Minor were oppressed by famine, and the ruling king, Atys, was forced to divide the population, sending half of it to find new lands abroad under the leadership of his son Tyrsenus. The emigrants sailed to Italy, and there Tyrsenus founded a new kingdom, whose inhabitants came to be called "Tyrsenoi," the Greek name for the Etruscans, in his memory. As Tyrsenus gave his name to the Tyrsenoi, so his brother Lydus did to the Lydians who remained, making the two peoples into kindred.[27]

As the Tyrsenoi were named for Tyrsenus, so at some point between the revival of Greek culture in the eighth century and the Persian Wars of the early fifth, the Greeks began to think of themselves as "Hellenes" and as descendants of an eponymous ancestor called Hellen.[28] This national or ethnic sense of "Hellene" was, however, inherently fluid. It is practically absent from the *Iliad* and totally so from the *Odyssey.* In religion, there was a "Hellenic Zeus" *(Zeus Hellēnios),* but he had no cult comparable to that of the supreme god of the Persians or the Israelites. Nor did the Greeks have any sacred text equivalent to the Jewish Law or the Christian scriptures, for Homer and Hesiod, though they supplied them with much of their mythology, were far from providing commandments or moral exemplars. In due course the term "Hellene" came to designate Greekness without reference to place or political system, and more and more acquired a sense of joint culture rather than one of joint kinship. This semantic shift was aided by the addition of another sense of *genos,* "type" or "species," which first appears in the fourth century.[29]

If the Greeks were slow to define themselves as Hellenes, they were no faster to achieve the notion of a collective "other." The word "barbarian" *(barbaros),* which later performed this function, is likewise almost absent from the Homeric poems, and its only use is to denote the Carians among the Trojan allies as "barbarous-voiced" *(barbarophōnos).* The shift from the meaning "unintelligible" to that of "non-Greek" was an easy one, with parallels in many other cultures.[30] Almost as soon as it was made, the word acquired connotations of inferiority, and in particular of "lack of civilization," "savagery." This sense is implied by Herodotus' observation on the Egyptians that "they call 'barbarians' all those who do not share their language" (for if this observation was merely about language, it would be tautologous), and it is even clearer in Thucydides' comments on the barbarity of Thracians and other tribes.[31] Thus the term "barbarian" was inherently as unstable as "Hellene," and the opposition between the two ideas which is so sharp in authors of the fifth and fourth century, especially with reference to the highly accomplished Persian empire, was not destined to endure.

A third category, which served to link the other two, was that of "philhellenes," cultivated non-Greeks whose admiration for Greek culture placed them, as it were, at the threshold of Hellenism, and sometimes carried them across it. An early example of such philhellenism is the Macedonian king Alexander I, a direct ancestor of Alexander the Great who is actually called "the Philhellene" in later literature.[32] While still a prince, Alexander tried to compete in the Olympic games, the most prestigious of the Greek athletic festivals. Challenged by his competitors on the ground that the competition "was not for barbarians but for

Greeks," he proved his Argive descent to the satisfaction of the board of umpires, the "Judges of the Greeks" *(Hellēnodikai)*. After his admission, he competed in the sprint *(stadion)* and tied for first place. Another member of the royal house must have competed in the Heraea of Argos some decades later, since a prize from the games has been found in the royal tombs at Vergina.[33]

One of the major functions of kinship diplomacy was to mediate between Hellenes and barbarians, usually bringing the latter into the camp of the former by rediscovering or "renewing" a common ancestry which, linking the parties by descent, also gave them a mutuality of interest. Alexander I may be said to have conducted his own kinship diplomacy when he persuaded the Hellenodikai to admit him to the Olympic games; his descendant, whose ancestors had worked patiently to be recognized as kinsmen of the Greeks, affirmed his own Greekness in part by propagandizing his respect for ties of *syngeneia*. One of the great achievements of such diplomacy was to convert the Roman republic, which at the time of Alexander the Great was still extending its power through the Italian peninsula, into a kindred nation, which eventually adopted Greek culture and in the Byzantine era became its chief vehicle.

Even when kinship diplomacy is not concerned with relations between Greeks and hellenized barbarians, it always has the function of providing a means of exchange between states, a mechanism whereby advantages of culture and descent can be converted into material and political ones. Usually the exchange is between a weaker party, often a city, and a stronger one such as a kingdom or a league. Sometimes the advantage gained was only the negative one of escaping destruction at the hands of an invading army, as in Diodorus' story of the Siboi. But sometimes great powers could be induced by considerations of kinship, not merely to spare a potentially hostile community, but to revive fallen ones or even to call them into existence, as Rome created the city of Aphrodisias in Caria. We will now see how these processes evolved, functioned, and were transformed by changes in the world that employed them.

2

THE BEGINNINGS

The Greek word *diplōma,* from which "diplomacy" comes, by a curious chance is first found in Roman contexts with the meaning of "pass" or "safe-conduct."[1] The etymological meaning is "folded object," and the form as opposed to the word is very ancient. Two (sometimes more) wooden boards ("tablets") were hinged together, their inner faces being treated with a special wax and framed with a raised edge to prevent damage to the writing. The scribe wrote by scratching the inner surfaces with a sharp stylus, and the resulting document could either be erased by melting the wax, or else preserved under seal, with a copy written, if necessary, on one of the outer faces. This is the form presumably taken by the passes and other *diplōmata* mentioned in our texts of the Roman period, as it is the form of the extant bronze certificates of service issued to soldiers in the auxiliary forces.[2]

The term *diplōma* continued in the Middle Ages to be used in the Latin West for folded documents of state, and from there passed into western vernaculars, the first attestation in English being from about 1645. The derivative noun, "diplomacy," was taken from French into English in the late eighteenth century, and hence the definition given a century later by the *Oxford Eng-*

lish Dictionary: "The management of international relations by negotiation; the method by which these relations are adjusted and
managed by ambassadors and envoys; the business or art of the di-
plomatist."[3]

The ancients had no equivalent to modern diplomacy, with its
elaborate array of procedures and definitions requiring trained,
professional experts. The Greeks, however, did slowly develop
something that is recognizable as diplomacy as they learned to
conduct negotiation, not only through written or oral messages
carried by human instruments, "heralds" *(kērykes)* or "messengers" *(angeloi),* but through persons entrusted with the power
both to carry messages and to treat with the other party.

Of the two great epics attributed to Homer, the *Iliad* certainly
shows communication being conducted through third parties,
though nothing that can be called diplomacy. Among the gods, it
is the king, Zeus, who mainly employs messengers, using for the
purpose Iris and, on one notable occasion, the personified Dream
(Oneiros).[4] Homer's word for messengers, *angelos,* is not native to
Greek, but a borrowing, related to a Persian word meaning "cou-
rier." From its sense of "divine messenger," it passed through
Christian Greek into modern languages as "angel."[5]

Similarly, among the Greek chiefs the highest one, Agamemnon, converses through messengers, who are either *angeloi* or
"heralds," *kērykes.* Thus in the first book he sends Talthybius
and Eurybates to reclaim Briseis from Achilles, who treats them
with politeness as "heralds [*kērykes*], messengers [*angeloi*] of Zeus
and men."[6] *Kēryx* is an Indo-European word already found in
Mycenaean Greek, and refers to the clarity of the speaker's voice.[7]
It emphasizes the physical act of proclamation, and the herald has
no power to reshape or add to his announcement. Chiefs other
than Agamemnon sometimes send messages through companions
or squires, but usually converse face to face.

By contrast with this instrumental form of communication, in
which the messengers are in effect animate objects, Homer describes a freer form in which the intermediary is empowered to
"persuade" the recipient, but such messengers are rulers chosen

by their peers. Thus, before the action of the *Iliad,* Menelaus and Odysseus came to Troy to win back Menelaus' runaway wife, Helen.[8] So also Telamonian Ajax and Odysseus are selected to go to Achilles' tent and to persuade him to rejoin the battle. They are preceded for safe conduct by "heralds," who are clearly regarded as inviolable.[9] In the final book, Priam goes in person on a mission to reclaim his son's body from Achilles, accompanied by Idaius, who is both driver and herald. Fearing that this may not be protection enough, Zeus sends the god Hermes to accompany Priam, rather as the heralds protect Ajax and Odysseus.[10]

If, as is usually supposed, the *Iliad* took written form in the eighth century and was substantially modified over the next two centuries, then it may give at least a rough idea of how communication was conducted between powers at the beginning of the archaic period. At the end of that period, by the time of the Persian Wars, something that can be called diplomacy had come into being, but the precise stages of its emergence cannot be followed. This was an age of poetry, not prose, and history as a form of literature did not come into existence until the end of it. Our chief witness, Herodotus, wrote in the third quarter of the fifth century, and though he has much to say about earlier periods, his principal subject is the Persian Wars, early in the same century, and his narrative does not become continuous before his account of the Ionian revolt about 500.

For Herodotus, the Homeric method of communicating, in which messengers are the prerogative of supreme rulers like Zeus and Agamemnon, is characteristic of the kings of Persia, who conducted all their business through "messengers" *(angeloi).*[11] Other "barbarian" rulers, however, had more flexible forms of communication well before the Persian Wars. Croesus the king of Lydia, seeking Greek allies against Cyrus, sends "messengers bearing gifts and asking for alliance, after he had ordered them as to what they ought to say." These clearly could not modify their message, but they must have had the freedom to make it as persuasive as possible.[12] An exchange a generation later implies a greater flexibility. In order to win to his side the ambitious

Polycrates of Samos, a Persian satrap of Sardis sends an unnamed Lydian with a "message" *(angeliē)* to him and invites the tyrant to send a trustworthy person back to test its truth. Polycrates appoints his scribe Maiandrius, who goes to Sardis, inspects the satrap's treasures, and returns to describe them to his master.[13]

By the last quarter of the sixth century, Greek communities began to entrust their negotiations to one or more representatives. In such contexts, Herodotus uses a new term, *presbys,* or the related verb *presbeuein,* derived from a root denoting precedence, and closely related to the noun *presbytēs,* "old man."[14] About 525 the exiled Samians convey their demands to the citizens of Siphnos through a delegation described by Herodotus both as "honored persons," *presbees,* and as "messengers," *angeloi.*[15] Some twenty years later the Spartans convene a conference of their allies to discuss the restoration of Hippias, the son of the Athenian tyrant Peisistratus. Herodotus identifies a certain Socles, the leader of the Corinthian delegation, as "having precedence from Corinth" *(presbeuōn apo Korinthou).* Socles argues passionately against any attempt by Sparta to introduce oligarchy among its democratic allies, and convinces all the other delegates present.[16] Whatever the truth of this account—and Herodotus has certainly taken the opportunity to give a ringing justification of democracy—it is likely enough that the rise of democratic states accompanied the emergence of diplomacy in its full form. "A certain political system," a veteran diplomat has said, "inevitably reflects itself in a certain type of diplomatic practice and theory."[17]

A functionary different from the *presbys* (later *presbeutēs*), or accredited envoy, and somewhat resembling the modern "honorary consul," is the *proxenos* ("defender of foreigners"), a citizen who because of his known ties or sympathies represents the interests of another city to his compatriots. Very little is heard of these people, however, in kinship diplomacy. Almost the only example is the ineffectual intervention of the wealthy Athenian Callias at a peace conference in 371.[18]

At some stage probably anterior to this democratic diplomacy, consciousness of shared descent between rulers and, later, communities began to engender kinship diplomacy of the kind observable in Diodorus' story of Alexander and the Siboi. A Homeric precedent, not concerned with kinship but with the closely related concept of guest-friendship *(xenia)*, is provided by an episode in the sixth book of the *Iliad,* the meeting of the Achaean hero Diomedes and the Lycian Glaucus. This is probably a late addition to the poem, perhaps from the sixth century, when the petty princes of the Xanthus valley, subject to Persia but strongly Hellenized, had grown so far in prosperity and power as to want to be able to claim a role in the Greek past.[19]

The two heroes meet in battle, and Diomedes, the first to speak, asks whether his adversary is a god or man; if a man, "come near, so that you may taste more quickly the end that is destruction." Glaucus begins his reply with a famous simile: "Bold-hearted son of Tydeus, why ask me my birth [*geneē*]? As the birth of leaves is, so is that of men. Some leaves the wind strews on the ground, others the burgeoning forest puts forth, and they are added in the season of spring: so the generation of men flourishes here and perishes there."[20] Glaucus goes on to tell how his grandfather Bellerophon was born in Ephyre in the Argolid, which later tradition identified with Corinth. By a folk-motif well known from the story of Joseph and Potiphar's wife, Anteia, the wife of king Proitus, accuses the hero to her husband of making advances to her. The king sends him off to his father-in-law, the ruler of Lycia, treacherously giving him a message contained in "baneful signs, inscribing many soul-destroying things in a folded tablet."[21] The Lycian king subjects him to a series of ordeals, which he overcomes with such success that the king gives him his daughter's hand and half his realm. From Bellerophon springs the royal line of Glaucus and his cousin, Sarpedon, the leader of the Lycian contingent at Troy.

Hearing of Glaucus' lineage, Diomedes recognizes him as an ancestral guest-friend *(xeinos)*. He in turn explains how Bellerophon had come to the house of his grandfather Oineus and been graciously entertained. Now, therefore, Glaucus is his guest-friend in Argos, and he himself will be Glaucus' when he comes to the land of Lycia.[22] After this mutual recognition, the heroes seal their private peace with a handshake and exchange gifts, Glaucus giving golden armor for Diomedes' bronze.

This incident has several curious ellipses, one of them the enigmatic "baneful signs." These are generally recognized, however, as a reference to some kind of writing—the first such reference in European literature—and the "folded tablet" as a reference to the hinged tablets known from Near Eastern art and archaeology.[23] In a curious way, Bellerophon is thus the first diplomat in European literature, though not the last to bear an order for his own death.

Despite the obliqueness of this story, several of its motifs recur, transformed, in later kinship diplomacy. One is the "wandering hero," here represented by Bellerophon banished from his native land. Another is contained in the ordeals which the hero must undergo before founding a dynasty or a community. A third is the motif of the "foreign prince," the hero of distant origin who marries the daughter of a local ruler. This motif was to be exploited by Vergil to explain the union of Trojans and Latins on Italian soil. A celebrated American counterpart is Pocahontas, "that most interesting of young squaws, or, to borrow the style of the day, of Indian princesses," whose marriage to an Englishman at Jamestown "secured a firm alliance between her tribesmen and the English."[24]

A modern reader readily hears the speech of Glaucus as an appeal to common humanity, to a wider sense of "birth" (*geneē*) than the aristocratic descent-group or house (*genos*) named after a single forefather. It is this latter type of kinship that is most prominent in the *Iliad,* where the patronymic, "son of Peleus," "son of Atreus," is often added to or even replaces the principal name. Kinship-groups such as the tribe (*phylon*) or clan (*phrētrē*) are mentioned but take no part in the action.[25] The Greeks in general are called variously "Achaeans," "Danaans," and "Argives"; the later term "Hellenes" is confined to a northern tribe among the followers of Achilles. The term "Panhellenes," which was to have a rich history, is once used together with "Achaeans" to refer to the Greeks in general.[26] There is no sign of a common kinship uniting all those on either the Greek or the Trojan side, but only of a common cause.

Such a kinship is, however, adumbrated by the poet Hesiod, who was often taken in antiquity to be a contemporary of Homer, though some of the poems attributed to him, like the Homeric epics, appear to have reached their final form only in the sixth century. The most personal of his poems, which may belong to the eighth or seventh century, is the *Works and Days,* and here he presents a scheme of five mortal races *(genē)* following in succession—gold, silver, bronze, "the divine race of hero-men" (including those who fought at Troy), and the fifth and last race of iron.[27] As the *Works and Days* presents a scheme classifying all mortals by successive races, so a poem attributed to Hesiod, the *Catalogue of Women,* classifies the Greeks and their major subdivisions. The "Hellenes" are descended from a single eponymous ancestor called Hellen, and their major genetic groups, each marked by their own dialect—Dorians, Ionians, and Aeolians—similarly descend each from one eponym, sons of Hellen (or, in the case of Ion, a grandson).[28]

The notion of a continuity between epic time and present time, implied by Hesiod's scheme of the five races, remains constant in Greek historiography, despite the tendency of its great practitioners to consider recent or contemporary history the worthiest subject of their study. For Herodotus there is no doubt either about such a continuity or about its power to influence the actions even of non-Greeks. According to a myth which is also embodied in Aeschylus' *Suppliants,* Inachus, the first king of Argos, had a daughter Io, with whom Zeus fell in love. Hera jealously transformed her into a cow, and after long wandering she regained her human shape in Egypt. Here she had two sons, Danaus and Aegyptus. The adult Danaus quarreled with his brother and returned to Greece with his fifty daughters. Here he became king of Argos, his ancestral city, and founded a line which led directly to Danaë and her son, the wandering hero Perseus.[29]

Herodotus begins his history with the wanderings of Io, reporting a Persian tradition whereby she came to Egypt in human shape, after being kidnapped by Phoenician sailors. Moreover, he himself has seen evidence of Egyptian belief in the myth of Danaus. He characterizes Amasis, the great pharaoh of the Twenty-sixth Dynasty, as "Greek-loving" *(philhellēn)*, the first appearance of this adjective in Greek. This monarch lavished gifts on the sanctuary of Athena at Lindos because "the daughters of Danaus [were] said to have founded it when running away from the sons of Aegyptus." If the story is not Herodotus' own invention, this is the first known time when such ties moved a philhellenic ruler to endow a Greek sanctuary.[30]

During Herodotus' Egyptian tour, he discovered in Chemmis—a town which still retains its ancient name as Achmim—a tradition that Danaus' descendant Perseus had come there in his pursuit of Medusa. Here he "recognized all his relatives," and in proof the citizens pointed out a temple of Perseus and his mother, and described the athletic competition *(agōn)* which they celebrated in Greek style. The language of "recognition" of relatives, supported by proofs drawn from local sights or customs, is another item that recurs in later diplomacy.[31]

A motif which resembles that of the wandering hero, in that it explains and justifies later connections between peoples, is that of three brothers who become the eponymous forefathers of kindred peoples.[32] Thus Caria in southwestern Asia Minor, in which Herodotus' own home city of Halicarnassus lay, had a communal shrine of Zeus at a city called Mylasa, which retains its name under the form Milas. Here three non-Greek peoples of western Asia Minor, Carians, Lydians, and Mysians, held an annual festival. According to Herodotus, obviously reporting local tradition, these peoples were descended from three brothers, Car, Lydus, and Mysus, sons of the Carian Zeus who was worshipped at the shrine.[33]

By Herodotus' account, kinship diplomacy of a kind began in the heroic age. By a common version of the myth of the Golden Fleece, the heroes aboard the *Argo* put in on the island of Lemnos, where they fathered children by the Lemnian women. This myth enters the historian's narrative when he tells, in great detail, the story of the founding of the first Greek settlement on African soil, Cyrene. In this part of his account, he claims to be following a version common both to Sparta and to its colonists on the island of Thera, the home of the first Greek settlers in Cyrene. Descendants of the Argonauts in the third generation came to Sparta after being driven from the island of Lemnos and encamped on Mount Taygetus. When the Spartans sent a "messenger" to ask their identity, the strangers appealed to them for protection as their "fathers." The Spartans yielded, "influenced most of all by the fact that the sons of Tyndareus [the heroes Castor and Pollux] had sailed on the *Argo*."[34] This story, like that of Perseus and the Chemmites, reads like the projection into mythic times of practices from Herodotus' own world.

Herodotus was born in a city of Dorian origins but Ionian culture, Halicarnassus, and the historiography of which he is regarded as the "father" came into existence in Ionia. It is therefore not surprising that this region is the first known to have used kinship diplomacy, when the Ionians rebelled against the Persians in 498. Herodotus' account of the revolt betrays his strong dislike of the Ionians, but there is no reason to disbelieve his account of their chief envoy, Aristagoras of Miletus, visiting Sparta and Athens in the winter of 499/8. In Sparta, Aristagoras produced a "bronze tablet on which the circuit of the whole world was inscribed, and all the sea and all the rivers." He also appealed to the Spartans as the leaders of Greece to help the Ionians, "men of the same blood," but in vain. Herodotus chances to use the same word for tablet, *pinax,* as Homer used for the "folded tablet" of Bellerophon. As that was the first reference to writing in European literature, so Aristagoras' "tablet" is the first reference to a map, and he is the first ambassador known to have carried a diplomatic instrument.[35]

In Athens Aristagoras was more successful. "The Milesians," so Herodotus reports him as claiming, "were colonists [*apoikoi*] of the Athenians, and it was proper that the Athenians with their great power should come to their aid."[36] Herodotus does not claim that kinship was Aristagoras' only plea. As happened in later ages, it was reinforced by arguments of expediency and national pride. The success of his appeal led to the burning of Sardis, the seat of the Persian satrap of Ionia, an act which in turn supplied the *casus belli* for Darius' armada against Attica, with its famous defeat at Marathon, and for Xerxes' invasion of Greece.

The mission of Aristagoras may be taken as the culmination of developments of the archaic period both in diplomacy and in the use of interstate kinship. Though in some ways he resembles the kingly envoys of Homer, at the same time he represents a whole people, adapts his message for his audience, and acts as a true diplomat. The success of his mission at Athens led ultimately to a new configuration of power in Greece and western Asia. The new or "classical" age of Greece, of which Athens rather than Ionia is the intellectual center, was also a new phase in kinship diplomacy.

3

THE CLASSICAL AGE

OF GREECE

The period between the Persian Wars and the death of Alexander was considered by later Greeks, by Romans, and by subsequent cultures as the classical age of Greece. It is flanked, at either end, by two great military campaigns possessing a curious symmetry. The invasion of Greece by Xerxes marked the farthest western reach of the Persian empire founded by Cyrus, while the overthrow of the Persian empire by Alexander of Macedon was the farthest extension of the Macedonian empire, and of Greek language and culture, into Asia. Among Greek cities, Athens combined power and the arts in an unprecedented flowering, which was to make it ever after the symbol of Greek culture, the "Hellas of Hellas."

The historian of diplomacy is largely dependent for the fifth century on Herodotus and on the exiled Athenian Thucydides, who are supplemented to some extent by later writers such as Diodorus of Sicily and Plutarch. For the first half of the fourth century, when Athens was in decline and the kingdom of Macedon on the eve of its great expansion, another Athenian exile, Xenophon, provides a continuous if unsatisfactory narrative. History is now overshadowed by oratory, which produces its greatest exponents, above all Isocrates and Demosthenes, both of them also active as diplomats, though in different ways. In the same century, documents in the form of inscriptions become increasingly frequent and informative.

For Herodotus, as we have seen, there is unquestioned historical continuity between the world of myth and his own world. Xerxes, on his march to the Hellespont, goes out of his way to ascend the citadel of Troy, where he worships Athena, the chief goddess of the city, and propitiates the fallen heroes.[1] This pilgrimage was to be made by other commanders eager to capture and exploit the Trojan legend, for example Alexander of Macedon.

The historian also reports a story about a message sent by Xerxes to Argos, though he does not vouch for its truth:

There is another story, repeated throughout Greece, that Xerxes sent a herald to Argos before he set out on his Greek campaign. This herald is supposed to have said on arrival in Argos, "Men of Argos, king Xerxes says this to you: we hold our ancestor to be Perses, the son of Perseus the son of Danaë, begotten by him from Andromeda the daughter of Cepheus. It would follow that we are your descendants. It is therefore proper neither for us to take the field against our ancestors, nor for you to come to the aid of others in opposition to us, but rather that you should stay quietly within your borders. If I achieve what I intend, I will value no people so highly as you." When the Argives heard this, it is said, they were greatly impressed by it, and at first they made no promise [to the Greeks] and asked for no share, but when the Greeks invited them in, only then did they ask to share in the leadership, knowing that the Spartans would not concede it, in order to have an excuse for remaining neutral.[2]

Though the story seems an obvious fiction, there is no reason to doubt that it was current, at least after the defeat of the Persians. Aeschylus alludes to their Argive ancestry in his play *The Persians*, produced only a few years after these events.³ Even if fictional, the story of Xerxes' approach to the Argives should mirror exchanges such as were already occurring between Greeks, and perhaps even between Greeks and barbarians. Perseus as a "wandering hero" linking Greeks and Iranians recurs later in the propaganda of the kings of Pontus.

Thucydides does not share Herodotus' readiness to trace chains of causation back to gods and heroes, or to regard them as intervening in contemporary affairs with dreams, visions, and omens. With some reluctance, however, he allows glimpses of diplomacy which invoked the mythic past, both during the fifty years that preceded the Peloponnesian War and during the war itself.⁴

About 458 the Spartans received an appeal from the "Dorians of the mother citadel [*mētropolis*]," that region in central Greece from which the Dorians were believed to have launched their southward migration. Attacked by their Phocian neighbors, these Dorians appealed to Sparta, which raised a large force from its Peloponnesian allies, forced the Phocians to withdraw, and then met the Athenians and their allies in an inconclusive battle at Tanagra. Thucydides does not give an express motivation for the Spartans' vigorous action, but several centuries later Diodorus of Sicily attributes it to ties of kinship *(syngeneia)* with the Dorians of the Metropolis.⁵

A recently published inscription, dated to the year 205, shows these same Dorians, now aided by the Aetolian League, making a widespread appeal to their Dorian and other kinfolk in order to rebuild the walls of their chief city, Cytenion. In this instance, when their aim is to influence the Lycian city of Xanthus, their ambassadors tell how a descendant of the Homeric Glaucus helped Aletes, a descendant of Heracles and the first Dorian king of Corinth, to win his throne. It is a reasonable inference that the "Dorians of the metropolis" had made similar appeals to ethnic solidarity when pressed by the Phocians in 458, as indeed the account of Diodorus implies.⁶

An ancient commentator observes that a passage in Thucydides' account of the year 430, the first full year of the

Peloponnesian War, represents the only occasion on which he goes into questions of myth.[7] Discussing an alliance between the Athenians and Sitalces, king of the Odrysian Thracians, the historian introduces an apparent digression on the king's ancestry. A well-known myth told how Pandion, a legendary king of Athens, had given his daughter Procne in marriage to a Thracian king called Tereus. Procne had then avenged Tereus' rape of her sister Philomela by killing Itys, the son she had had by Tereus. Thucydides' only purpose in alluding to the myth seems to be the negative one of denying any connection between the mythical Tereus and the historical Teres, the father of Sitalces, and it is natural to suspect that he is covertly criticizing some contemporary view, perhaps one expressed in literature. Now the alliance between Athens and Thrace was mediated by a Greek from Abdera on the Thracian coast, a certain Nymphodorus, whose sister had married Sitalces. Abdera was a colony of Teos in Ionia, though it attributed its original foundation to Heracles.[8] In later diplomacy, mythic precedents are often invoked to justify parallel actions in the present, and Nymphodorus seems to have exploited the myth of Tereus and Procne as a precedent for Sitalces' alliance with Athens, the mother city of the Ionians. In some form flattering to Sitalces, the myth may also have occurred in contemporary drama; Sophocles is known to have written a *Tereus,* though its date is uncertain.[9]

Though reluctant to admit myth into his narrative, Thucydides is very attentive to the contrast between the two leading kinship-groups (*genē*) of contemporary Greece, Dorians and Ionians, at least as a factor in the speeches and propaganda of the protagonists, Athens and Sparta, and their allies. For this purpose he uses the term that is standard in later periods, *syngeneia,* or a variant, *to syngenes*.[10] Likewise, he gives full weight to the colonization of the archaic period and to the links of obligation that bound mother cities and their settlements abroad, for example in the quarrel between Corinth, Corcyra, and Epidamnus that directly ignited the war in 431. But his mistrust of such links appears from the way in which he illustrates their rupture under the force of expediency or fear. The Melians hoped in vain that the Spartans would help them "because of our kinship"; those who sided with Athens in the Sicilian expedition did so "not in accordance with justice and kinship" but from political calculation.[11]

Finally, in discussing the diplomacy of the Peloponnesian War Thucydides sometimes alludes to considerations of kinship or of "intimacy," *oikeiotēs*. After the disaster of Sphacteria in 425, the Spartans approach the Athenians through ambassadors, offering peace, alliance, and in general a state of "full friendship and intimacy [*philia pollē kai oikeiotēs*] with each other."[12] Here the latter term cannot denote a sort of kinship, and *oikeiotēs* must be a state brought about by the signing of peace, not something already in existence. In the following year the cities of Sicily hold a conference to discuss the perceived threat of invasion from Athens. The chief delegate from Syracuse, Hermocrates, urges his fellow Sicilians not to be lulled by considerations of descent *(genos)*. Those of Chalcidic origin (colonists from the Ionian city of Chalcis in Euboea) "must not suppose themselves safe because of their Ionian kinship . . . No shame follows when those who are close [*oikeioi*] yield to one another, either a Dorian to a Dorian or a Chalcidian to a kinsman [*syngenēs*]." The logic of the argument requires that *oikeios* be a more comprehensive term than *syngenēs,* embracing all those whom proximity brings together, and not only those who are related.[13]

In the generation after Thucydides, Xenophon also knows of appeals to kinship in diplomacy. One such involves his own experience. The "Ten Thousand," an army of Greek mercenaries hired by the Persian pretender Cyrus, struggled back to Europe after the failure of their campaign, and after crossing the Bosporus began to negotiate with a Thracian princeling called Seuthes, who wished to use the remaining Greeks for his own dynastic ambitions. Xenophon as their leader led the negotiations, and as a historian he gives a cool, amused portrait of the barbarian prince, who professed implicit faith in the kinship of Thracians and Athenians in order to win over his Athenian interlocutor.[14]

In his chief historical work, the *Hellenica,* Xenophon follows the example of Thucydides in his reluctance to admit divine causation, though he allows speakers within his text to do so.[15] One such is a wealthy Athenian, Callias the son of Hipponicus, a member of the *genos* of Heralds *(Kērykes)*, which traditionally supplied one of the chief officeholders of the Eleusinian Mysteries. Callias also had a family tradition of sympathy toward Sparta, of which he was the resident spokesman *(proxenos)*. At a peace congress held at Sparta in 371, he invokes the mythic history of his own family to justify peace between Sparta and Athens:

> It is not right for us even to take up arms against each other, for they say that the first outsiders [*xenoi*] to whom my family's ancestor, Triptolemus, displayed the secret ritual objects were Heracles, your originator [*archēgetēs*], and the Dioscuri, your fellow citizens; and it was to the Peloponnese that he first gave the seed of Demeter's grain. How can it be right, then, for you ever to come and ravage the grain of those who gave you seed, or for us not to wish that those we gave it to should have the greatest possible plenty?[16]

Though the historian wants to bring out Callias' self-importance and family pride, there is no reason to suppose that he has attributed to him arguments which were never made. "However basic truths in diplomacy may be commonly recognized and agreed to tacitly," it has been said, "myths, attitudes and postures have often to be maintained even when the majority can see through the fiction."[17]

Immediately after the congress at Sparta, there began a chain of events in the Peloponnese which was destined to transform the region politically. The peace of 371 in fact led immediately to war between Sparta and Thebes, in the course of which the Thebans invaded the Peloponnese and brought about the foundation of two new cities as counterweights to Sparta, Messene in the southwest and Megalopolis as the capital of Arcadia, the land-locked region occupying the center of the peninsula.[18] These events were accompanied by diplomacy no less than by war, and the Arcadian participants, drawing on their own legends, were in turn to create links of memory for future generations.

A tangible expression of the defeat of the Spartans in 369 is a large monument at Delphi, described by the traveler Pausanias in the imperial period and still partly preserved.[19] It was a large statue-base set up by the Arcadians and carrying statues of Apollo (the presiding god of Delphi), Victory, and a series of figures from Arcadian legend—the nymph Callisto, who in union with Zeus had given birth to the eponymous hero Arcas, and his three sons Elatus, Apheidas, and Azan (another example of the scheme of three brothers). In these claims of antiquity and independence, the implied link with Delphi is essential, and the cardinal figure appears to be the first-named son of Arcas, Elatus. As often, Pausanias provides the key. Elatus came from Arcadia with an army to help the Delphians who were under attack from a hostile tribe. Thereafter he settled with his followers in central Greece and founded the city called Elatea in Locris, which had close ties to Delphi (a variant of the "helping hero" motif, whereby the hero acts not alone, but as the leader of an army).[20]

These events were to find an echo a hundred and fifty years later, when the city of Magnesia on the Maeander conducted a diplomatic campaign on behalf of its local Artemis and her festival. The Magnesians had their own long mythical history, which allegedly began with the sending out of colonists from Delphi.[21] This Delphian connection seems to have been the basis of their appeal to cities of the Arcadian league as "relatives and friends" *(syngeneis kai philoi),* and these in their turn passed decrees of which only that of the Megalopolitans is preserved. They justified their assent to the Magnesians' request by recalling a favor which they had done to the Arcadians at the time of the founding of Megalopolis. These had sent a deputation to their Asian "kinsmen" in Magnesia, asking for money to help fortify the new foundation. Even though the Magnesians were still under Persian rule, they raised a huge gift, worth three hundred gold staters or "Darics," about 2.5 kilograms in nearly pure gold. The text does not say by what plea the Arcadian ambassadors obtained this gift, and no doubt the politics of the 360s played a part, but one argument must surely have been the mythic link between Magnesia and the Arcadians. This exchange of embassies and favors anticipates the diplomatic campaigns of Greek cities in the Hellenistic period.

The founding of Megalopolis had a curious coda, which again is known only from Pausanias, and may be apocryphal. Certain of the Arcadian cities refused to join the new city, one of them a certain Trapezus. This was later claimed by the more famous Trapezus on the Black Sea, the medieval Trebizond, as its metropolis. Rather than merging their identity in the "Great City," the citizens of the Arcadian Trapezus set sail for northern waters, where their kinsmen in the other Trapezus gave them shelter. This story looks like an invention of the Anatolian Trapezus, concocted when the city had risen to prominence and begun to need a respectable pedigree. Nonetheless, the duty of mother cities and colonies to help each other in time of crisis is well attested in later centuries.[22]

No Greek colony had a more complex web of tradition around its origins than Cyrene, the first Greek colony on the soil of Africa. Like other colonies, for instance Abdera in Thrace, it traced its beginnings back to the heroic age, to the voyage of the *Argo*. In historic time, it was founded in the seventh century from the island of Thera, which in its turn had been settled by Dorians from the Peloponnese. By the fourth century, Cyrene far outstripped the mother city in wealth and prestige, and an inscription discovered there in the 1920s is the first contemporary one to reflect the workings of kinship diplomacy.[23]

The issue was the claim of native Theraeans resident in Cyrene to enjoy full citizen rights. The inscription shows that the Theraeans of the mother city had approached Cyrene, asking it to give the immigrants their full rights, and for the purpose had cited an oath allegedly sworn by the original founders. The relevant provision states that if the colony is successful, "any relative [oikeios] who later sails to Libya shall enjoy citizenship and honors, and be assigned a share of unowned land." The authenticity of this oath is doubtful, all the more since there was a lively business in patriotic forgeries about this time.[24] For the present purpose it matters more that the text shows diplomats reaching back to the age of the semilegendary Battus, the originator *(archēgetēs)* of the colony. Like the appeal of the Megalopolitans to Magnesia, therefore, the Cyrenaean inscription is a forerunner of Hellenistic diplomacy.

Kinship diplomacy, which begins to make its first appearance in the archaic period, has thus reached a stable form and developed much of its vocabulary by the end of the classical one. In matters of consequence, such as the Sicilian resistance to Athens, it continues to be a device which needs reinforcement by other pleas—expediency, prestige, self-justification. But a new aspect already starts to appear, the use of kinship to obtain assistance in the form of loans, privileges, and the like. That is, this type of diplomacy has already become a means of exchange between states of unequal wealth or power, a way of converting the spiritual and emotional debt owed to founders and benefactors into material advantage.

Though classical Greece is easily thought of as the golden era of the *polis,* the institution of kingship, familiar from the Homeric poems, persisted in a curious double form in Sparta, and also in lands on the borders of the Greek world. One of these kingdoms, the Macedonian, was to bring the classical period to a close by the actions of Philip II and his son Alexander III, while the neighboring kingdom of Epirus to the northwest began to intervene in Sicily and Italy. Long before, however, the Greeks had learned to involve both these kingdoms, as they had the kingdom of Thrace, in the net of mythical kinship.

4

TWO NORTHERN

KINGDOMS

$\mathscr{T}$he distinction between Greeks and barbarians, easily as it seemed to characterize such great conflicts as the Persian Wars, raised the problem of liminal peoples who were neither in nor out of the Greek family, and yet such near neighbors as to demand some kind of recognition. Two, closely interconnected by their history and geography, inhabited the kingdoms of Macedon and Epirus, though both populations in fact consisted of a number of related tribes. Macedon was in due course to transform the political face of Asia, at the time acting as a carrier of Greek language and culture, while the ambitions of Epirus began the landslide that ended with Rome's supremacy over the Mediterranean.

Of the two kingdoms, Macedonia was strategically if not geographically closer to mainland Greece, and its language too appears to have been a form of Greek, though whether the Macedonians were Greeks was disputed even in antiquity.[1] From at least the sixth century, the ruling house claimed descent from Heracles and kinship with Argos in the Peloponnese. Contested from the very first, these claims became impossible to gainsay when asserted by Philip II in the mid-fourth century. His son Alexander could boast not only Heraclid ancestry but also descent from

Achilles and Andromache through his mother, Olympias, a daughter of Neoptolemus I of Epirus.

The link of the Macedonian royal house with Argos is variously explained, but Herodotus' version is the earliest known, and its evident borrowings from folklore have the look of authentic tradition.[2] Perdiccas, the founder of the royal house, descended from Temenus, a Heraclid and the first Dorian king of Argos. Expelled from Argos with his brothers Aerops and Gauanes, Perdiccas at first served in the household of a Macedonian king. When portents foretold his greatness, the king expelled the brothers and tried to kill them, but after many adventures they conquered the land for themselves. This myth, besides creating the vital link with Heracles, the prince of Greek heroes, and with Argos of mythic fame, also contains a stock motif of kinship-myth, that of the three brothers who represent three cognate tribes. As Perdiccas stands for Macedon, so does Aerops for the lesser kingdom of the Lyncestae and Gauanes for that of the Elimiotae.[3]

The first Macedonian king who is more than a name, Alexander I later called "the Philhellene," interests Herodotus because of his role in the Persian Wars, and perhaps because of his son and successor, Perdiccas II. Herodotus expresses no doubt that the Macedonian royal house was of Greek origin, and he is the source of the story, already mentioned, of Alexander's successful attempt to compete at the Olympic games. Thucydides too has no doubt that the kings of Macedon were Temenids from Argos.[4]

Both Alexander and his son Perdiccas had frequent contacts with cities of Greece. According to Herodotus, Alexander made a secret visit to the Greek camp before Plataea, and gave the Greeks crucial information about the plans of the Persian general, Mardonius, asserting that he himself was "a Greek by descent [genos] and would not wish to see Greeks no longer free but enslaved."[5] This romantic tale may be fiction, and a more telling item, because so casually introduced, occurs in Thucydides. Sparta and Argos made a treaty in the winter of 418/17, and immediately began trying to bring Perdiccas over from the Athenian side to their own. The king "did not immediately desert the Athenians, but began to think about doing so when he saw that the Argives had, since he himself was Argive by origin."[6] Thucydides' language shows that the supposed kinship with Argos influenced the king's policy, and it can surely be inferred that the Spartan and Argive ambassadors appealed to his descent from Heracles and the Argive Temenus.

From 413 to 399 the Macedonian throne was held by Perdiccas' son Archelaus. Ambitious to strengthen and consolidate his kingdom, Archelaus also took the role of patron of Greek culture. Among the visitors to his court was the aged Euripides, who wrote in his honor a highly successful play in which the hero was a namesake of the king. This ancestral Archelaus was a son of Temenus, and was banished from Argos by his brothers, thus becoming a "wandering hero." In this role he eventually came to Macedon, where he founded the Argead line. This version of the king's Temenid descent must have been either invented by the poet or else borrowed by him from the Macedonian court. Euripides, who also proclaimed the Trojan origins of the royal house of Epirus, is thus a forerunner of those poets and historians who elaborated the ancestral myths of Hellenistic states, sometimes serving as ambassadors in their own right.[7]

Philip II, a descendant of Alexander I by a collateral line, established Macedon as a Mediterranean power and prepared the assault on Persia which was to be carried out by his son, Alexander III or "the Great." Of his several literary portraits, the most influential one is drawn by his enemy Demosthenes, whose Athenian outlook is embodied in a famous gibe: "Not a Greek or having anything in common with the Greeks, not even a barbarian from somewhere it is decent to mention, but a damned Macedonian, from a country where up to now you couldn't even buy a decent slave."[8] Behind Demosthenes' taunt there lies not only the long history of Macedonian relations with Greek cities, but a propaganda offensive conducted both by Philip and by pro-Macedonian writers.

While the question of Macedonian Hellenism went back well

over a century, it was sharpened by a series of successes in the mid-340s—Philip's destruction of Olynthus in 348, his termination of the Sacred War in 346, his consequent succession to the two votes of the Amphictyonic Council previously held by Phocis, and his presidency of the Pythian games in the same year.[9] Two Athenian authors, friendly to Philip but not to each other, preserve something of the ethnic debates which these and later events aroused—Isocrates and Speusippus, the nephew of Plato.

Isocrates' *Philip* is an open letter to the king written in 346, when the settlement of the Sacred War had not yet turned Athenian opinion against the recently concluded peace between Athens and Philip, the so-called Peace of Philocrates. Isocrates' chief purpose is to urge Philip "to promote concord among the Greeks and a campaign against the barbarians," that is, to turn his power and energies eastward, to the liberation of Asian Greeks and to vengeance for the wrongs done to all Greeks by Persia. Isocrates' mythical arguments center on two figures, Heracles, the ancestor of the Temenid house, and his descendant, not named by the author, who founded the royal line of Macedon.[10] Heracles is more than the hero of superhuman strength and endurance familiar from earlier poetry. He is a moral exemplar, who made the world safe for Greek civilization by his tireless travels and his victories over monsters and tyrants.

Isocrates lays special emphasis on one of the hero's less-celebrated exploits, his capture of Troy after a campaign of a mere ten days. Thus Heracles becomes a prefiguration of the role which Isocrates envisages for Philip: "Seeing Greece full of wars, internal quarrels, and many other evils, he brought these to an end, reconciled the cities to one another, and showed posterity with whom and against whom they should make war."[11] Philip also inherits the honor which his ancestor earned from the leading cities of Greece, notably Athens, which protected his descendants from the tyrant Eurystheus. As a descendant of Heracles, so the orator argues, he cannot be suspected of intending to harm the Greeks.[12] Isocrates does not call Philip a Greek outright, but rather a "philhellene," and the orator confines his use of the word "kinship" *(syngeneia)* to express the relationship between authentic Greeks. Nonetheless, his use of Heracles must reflect an argument actually made in the contemporary diplomacy of kinship. As the founder of Philip's line *(archēgos tou genous),* Heracles both creates a link between Philip and Greece and provides a model to guide the king's actions.[13]

The same is true of Heracles' descendant, the founder of the Macedonian royal house. Aspiring to higher power than he could attain at Argos, "alone of the Hellenes" this man chose to rule over an alien race. Unlike others—Isocrates is thinking of such famous houses as the Atreids of Mycenae—he was thus able to bequeath power to his own posterity.[14] The expression which Isocrates uses for the Macedonians, "not of the same race" *(oukh homophylon),* is no mere euphemism for "barbarian." A compound of the prefix meaning "same" or "shared" and (probably) the noun *phylon,* "kind," it assigns them to a category of peoples neither Greek nor non-Greek, just as Philip is a descendant of Heracles and of the first Macedonian king, and yet not to be called Greek. Thus the founder's position as a Hellene ruling a nation to which he does not belong prefigures the role of Philip, a philhellene who will lead the Greeks against the true barbarians, the Persians.[15]

A riposte to Isocrates survives under the name of Speusippus, the nephew of Plato, and though its authenticity has been questioned it is surely genuine.[16] Apparently written about four years after the orator's *Philip,* it is intended to outbid that inveterate critic of Plato's Academy rather than to further any political message, but is still revealing for the use of myth in relations between states. The author's chief ally against Isocrates is an otherwise unknown historian, Antipater of Magnesia.[17] Whereas Isocrates' research *(historia)* is dismissed in a single line, Antipater is praised for his "credible myths" *(mythoi axiopistoi).* Since Speusippus' uncle Plato had mounted a famous attack on the myths narrated by Homer and other poets, the term *axiopistos,* literally "creditworthy," was necessary to distinguish Antipater's myths from those of the usual kind. This compound adjective perhaps derives from the circle of Socrates.[18]

The central figure in Antipater's myth is of course Heracles. Isocrates had overlooked a tale which showed the familiarity *(oikeiotēs)* between Heracles and Athens. The hero when visiting Athens had wished to be initiated into the Mysteries, but a law forbade the initiation of strangers *(xenoi)*, and Pylius therefore adopted Heracles as his own son. This story, known only from much later authors, illustrates exactly the sense and the importance of the elusive "familiarity" in relations between states. Speusippus could not claim kinship between Heracles and Athens, but used instead the closest relationship possible.[19]

Despite the differences from Isocrates, Speusippus resembles him in using myth, not as a dead link to the past, but as a dynamic example applicable to the present. Several of his arguments are drawn from cities which Philip had seized from Athens or from the Athenian alliance, Olynthus, Potidaea, Amphipolis. In these very regions, so Antipater had conveniently found, Heracles overthrew tyrants, giving their lands to be held in trust until his descendants could claim them.[20] Since Philip had saved these same lands from usurpation, as a descendant of Heracles he was free to dispose of them as he pleased.

While it is not known that Philip or his ambassadors used such arguments, it is certain that Heracles was prominent in his propaganda and appears frequently on his coins. The king's coinage also shows the head of Zeus and a group of horsemen holding a palm, a clear reference to his victories at Olympia. Both symbols are again connected with Heracles, who was said to have founded the original Olympics in honor of his divine father.[21] Like Euripides at the court of Archelaus, Antipater was probably not inventing his own myths, but using ones supplied to him by interested informers.

Alexander, who succeeded Philip in 336, could claim Argive descent on both sides. His father was a Temenid, while Olympias was a daughter of Neoptolemus I of Epirus, so that their son embodied both sides in the conflict immortalized by Homer. His conquest of Persia opened new fields for learned speculation, and new lands for Greek and Macedonian settlement, and this wave of colonization was in turn to create yet further links of kinship.

Already by the time of Xerxes' visit in 480, Homer's Troy had become a potent symbol, a focus for varying and sometimes conflicting claims. The Trojan war could be treated, as it was by Herodotus and Simonides, as a prefiguration of the great struggle between Greece and Persia, though Homer had treated both sides as equally heroic, speaking the same language and obeying the same code of honor. Just as Xerxes had "gone up" to the citadel of Ilium before crossing the Dardanelles in 480, so now Alexander "went up" after crossing them in the other direction, and, like the Persian king, made sacrifice to Athena and funeral offerings to the fallen heroes. Alexander, however, could claim descent from the "best of the Achaeans," Achilles, and his court historians duly reported how he honored his ancestor's gravestone and prayed to Priam not to be angry with a descendant of Neoptolemus.[22]

Another gesture of Alexander, even if with little consequence at the time, was still an omen of the future. According to the Augustan geographer Strabo, the king "was moved to provide for [the Ilians] in accordance with a renewal of kinship, and also as a lover of Homer." He thus gave fiscal and political advantages to the city, and "promised to make it great, to make the sanctuary very celebrated, and to institute sacred games."[23] Strabo's expression, "renewal of kinship" *(ananeōsis syngeneias),* is the same as the one used by his older contemporary Diodorus to describe the exchange between the Siboi and Alexander of Macedon. This is the first known occasion on which such a "renewal" leads a monarch to benefit a city, and such "renewals," not necessarily leading to benefits or gifts, are frequent in the diplomacy of the Hellenistic period.

As Alexander left Europe behind him, his Trojan ancestors shrank in importance, and others came to the fore, notably Heracles, to whom he sacrificed immediately after crossing the Hellespont.[24] After serving to justify Philip's conquests in Thrace, Heracles could now be seen as Alexander's predecessor in Asia, both as a sacker of cities and, perhaps more importantly, as a campaigner against distant and strange peoples. This connection also explains the tradition that the Amazons, mythical opponents of

Heracles, sought to negotiate with Alexander.[25] As the Trojans had profited from their association with Homer, so the city of Mallus in Cilicia, founded by the Argive seer Amphilochus, profited from its link with Heracles. Alexander "remitted the tribute which the citizens paid to Darius, since the Mallotae were colonists from Argos, and he claimed to descend from the Heraclidae of Argos."[26]

The farther Alexander proceeded into Asia, the rarer became the authentic traces of Greek culture, but he and his staff were no less alert than Herodotus had been a century or so earlier to find traces of Greek gods and heroes in strange lands. Thus two of his Thessalian officers, Medeius of Larissa and Cyrsilus of Pharsalus, concluded that the Armenians were actually Thessalian. An ancient town of Thessaly, Armenion, had been founded by an eponym called Armenus, who then followed another local hero, Jason, on his quest for the Golden Fleece. After Jason's marriage with the Colchian princess Medea, Armenus accompanied him on a military campaign into the region later called Armenia, and his own followers colonized the region. Corroborating evidence came from the similarity between Armenian and Thessalian dress, and the skill of both peoples at horseback-riding. Just as the Medes were named after Medus, the son of Jason and Medea, so the Armenians were kin to the Thessalians and descended from a follower of Jason.[27]

In this scheme, publicized by one or both of these officers in a history, familiar motifs of kinship recur—the wandering hero who marries a foreign princess, as Bellerophon married a princess of Lycia; the ancestor who gives his name to cities and peoples; the proofs of kinship drawn from evidence such as dress and local habits. In all this, the two historians were perhaps using Armenus as a kind of personal paradigm, as Isocrates had used Heracles and the founder of the Macedonian royal house for Philip. Just as Armenus had followed Jason into Armenia, so they themselves had followed Alexander into the east.

At the farthest stage of his campaign, in the valleys of the Cophen (Kabul) and Indus (Sindh) Rivers, Alexander and his staff were in a region perhaps already associated in Greek myth with Dionysus and Heracles, and certainly possessing a large array of gods in whom it was easy to see Greek equivalents. Dionysus was not so clearly connected with Alexander as Heracles, but he too was a son of Zeus and so of kindred stock, and there seems no doubt that the historical tradition associating him with Alexander goes back to the king himself.[28]

Even here, then, there was room for "the renewal of kinship," and court historians recorded at least two instances. In what is now northern Afghanistan, Alexander was approached by envoys from a city whose local god he and his companions recognized as Dionysus. The king duly identified it as Nysa, the legendary birthplace of the god, and gave it freedom and other benefits. Farther south, in the modern Punjab, Alexander met the ambassadors of the Siboi, whose dealings with the king we have already considered as a paradigm of kinship diplomacy.[29]

By coincidence, the last years of Alexander were exactly the time when Greek cities began to use the word "kinship" (syngeneia) in their inscribed documents. The earliest such text is a decree of Priene dated to the early 320s. As an Ionian city, Priene claimed kinship with Athens, the spiritual home of the Ionians and the reputed origin of their migration to Asia, and in the decree the citizens resolve to send a delegation and a panoply (suit of full armor) to Athens at every celebration of the Great Panathenaea "as a memorial of the original kinship and friendship between us and them." By contrast, a decree of Athens, passed some twenty years later in honor of another Ionian city, Colophon, speaks of the inhabitants as "colonists" but refers only to the intimacy (oikeiotēs) between the two cities. This reluctance of Athens to acknowledge kinship even with its mythical colonies appears to have been deliberate policy.[30]

As the royal house of Macedon claimed descent from Heracles, so the royal house of the Molossians, the dominant tribe of the Epirote federation, did from Achilles and his son, variously called Pyrrhus or Neoptolemus. As the story is told by Pindar, Neoptolemus did not return to his ancestral Thessaly, but instead settled in Epirus with Andromache, the widow of Hector, as his captive bride. Here he founded a line of kings which was both Greek and Trojan by descent, though their name "Aeacids," deriving from the grandfather of Achilles, stresses their Hellenism. Euripides gives a different version, in which Neoptolemus pays the just penalty for his murder of Priam, and Andromache marries one of the king's surviving sons, Helenus. A contemporary of Euripides, the historian Hellanicus of Lesbos, linked Epirus to Troy in another way, asserting that Aeneas stayed among the Molossians before crossing to Italy. Behind these legends of a Trojan connection with Epirus lie actual place-names of the region, Troia and Pergamis. These are probably authentic local names which from an early time gave the region a place in poems about the return home of Homeric heroes *(nostoi)*. As in Lycia, these traditions may have been invented, or at least exploited, by local chiefs with Hellenic pretensions.[31]

The first Molossian king who is more than a name, the late-fifth-century Tharyps, is said to have "adorned his kingdom with Hellenic customs, literature, and laws," but it is unknown whether Greek states such as Athens exploited mythic links in their dealings with him.[32] The pride of the fourth-century Aeacid kings in their heroic ancestry is shown by their names: Neoptolemus I the grandson of Tharyps; his nephew Aiacides, who ruled briefly after the death of his cousin Alexander of Macedon; and Aiacides' son Pyrrhus, who called one of his own sons Helenus.[33] A notable monument from Athens shows the good relations between that city and an exiled Epirote king, Arybbas the younger brother of Neoptolemus I, whom Philip II of Macedon had driven from the throne. The relief proudly commemorates Arybbas' victories in the chariot and horse races at the two chief festivals of the Greeks, the Olympia and Pythia.[34]

While Alexander was campaigning in Asia, his kinsman and brother-in-law, Alexander of Epirus, made an expedition into southern Italy. During this foray he made a treaty with Rome, the first Greek-speaking monarch to enter into relations with the power now coming to dominate Italy. Too little is known about

Alexander's expedition to tell whether it involved claims of kinship between the Molossian king and his south Italian allies, as did the similar campaign of Pyrrhus a generation later.[35]

In the case of Pyrrhus, king of Epirus from 297 to 272, there is no doubt of the exploitation of mythic links for purposes of advertisement and diplomacy, and of their propagation by artfully chosen historians. The best known of these is a certain Proxenus, who luckily discovered that Neoptolemus, the son of Achilles, had married a certain Lanassa, a descendant of Heracles and namesake of Pyrrhus' wife. Such a discovery recalls the researches of the historian Antipater praised by Speusippus fifty years before.[36]

Pyrrhus' campaigns in Italy and Sicily from 280 to 275 are a turning point in Mediterranean history and presage an ever-closer connection between its eastern and western halves in the centuries to come. The immediate cause was an appeal for help from the Spartan colony of Tarentum in southern Italy. The Tarentine ambassadors, according to Pausanias, "told [Pyrrhus] about Italy, saying that in its fertility it matched all of Greece, and that it was sacrilegious for him to dismiss friends and suppliants who had come to him at this moment. When the ambassadors said all this, Pyrrhus was reminded of the capture of Troy, and he expected he would enjoy the same success if he went to war, for he would be a descendant of Achilles fighting against colonists of the Trojans." This account is precisely borne out by coins which the king later issued in southern Italy. The obverse shows the head of Achilles; the reverse shows his mother, Thetis, carrying newly forged armor to her son at Troy. (See Figure 1.)[37] Despite Pausanias, Pyrrhus must have been too conscious of his ancestry to need "reminding." This term surely covers a "renewal" in which the Tarentines appealed to the role of Achilles at Troy.

To the same context may belong an oracle allegedly given to Pyrrhus either by Apollo of Delphi or by Zeus of Dodona, though since the latter shrine had been lavishly endowed by the king and lay within his kingdom, it is perhaps the more likely. The poet Ennius gives it in Latin form, and with a syntactical ambiguity which is hardly possible in Greek: "I declare, descendant

Figure 1. Coin of Pyrrhus, king of Epirus,
showing Thetis carrying armor to Achilles

of Aeacus, that you can defeat the Romans," or alternatively, "that the Romans can defeat you." Though Ennius' version of the oracle must be his own, it is fully possible that Pyrrhus consulted Dodona when planning his attack on the Romans, and that the god's reply proclaimed his descent from Aeacus and Achilles.[38]

Two years after his arrival in Italy, responding to a request from the Greek cities of Sicily, Pyrrhus undertook to expel the Carthaginians from the island. Just as the Romans could be represented as descendants of the non-Greek Trojans, so even more could Carthaginians be branded with associations of Persia and other barbarian enemies of Greece. For this purpose, Pyrrhus adroitly used Heracles as his forebear rather than Achilles, in effect making the same shift as Alexander of Macedon had done in Asia.

One incident shows the king using his Heraclid ancestry much as Speusippus had urged Philip II to use his. An ancient tradition held that the hero had once visited Sicily and been challenged by the fearsome wrestler Eryx, the eponym of the city of the same name in the northwestern part of the island. He defeated him, and left his lands to his own descendants. In 510 a Spartan prince,

47

Dorieus, was persuaded by this legend to found a colony here called Heraclea, but it was wiped out by the Carthaginians and the neighboring Segestans. About to begin his assault on Eryx, Pyrrhus now called on Heracles to "show him a worthy champion of his house [*genos*] and of its possessions to the Greeks living in Sicily," and after taking the city paid his vow with lavish sacrifices and contests. By a curious confluence of myths, Eryx was also associated with the wanderings of Aeneas, and in the First Punic War was to be bitterly contested between Romans and Carthaginians.[39]

The exploits of Alexander of Macedon, and perhaps also of Pyrrhus, find an echo in an enigmatic Greek poem which also predicts the power of Rome, the *Alexandra* of Lycophron of Chalcis. The date is disputed, but is probably about the second quarter of the third century.[40] The poem is cast in the form of a prophecy of Cassandra (the "Alexandra" of the title) as she foresees the doom both of the Trojans and of their conquerors, the Greeks. She heralds the glory of descendants of Troy, "who will win the crown of the first spoils with their spears, receiving the rule and sole mastery of land and sea." Near the end of the poem, she predicts Alexander's overthrow of the Persians, who are his "kinsmen" in that they too trace their descent to Argos. "Six generations later a kinsman of mine, a true contender with [Alexander], bringing to battle the valor of his spear and coming to an exchange of sea and earth, will be praised as foremost among his friends, taking the spear-won pick of the spoils."[41] Whoever this person is, the poet seems clearly to see a crisis of Mediterranean history in terms of mythic kinships. Argos, the center of the coalition against Troy, has now perished in the fall of its two great heirs, Macedonians and Persians. At last the royal house of Troy, of which Cassandra is a doomed remnant, will have its revenge through its descendants, and they will win "sole mastery of land and sea."

An Alexandrian poem of proverbial obscurity might be thought to have little to do with the politics of state. But in antiquity poets and other artists did more than supply the material with which diplomats worked. They also articulated ways in which relations between states could be viewed in literate society. Whatever Lycophron's precise date, whether of the early third or the early second century, he lived in an age dominated by the great powers which had divided up Alexander's empire, when lesser powers, such as cities and leagues, could still retain a measure of independence by war and diplomacy. The diplomacy of kinship was now entering on its most active phase.

5

CITIES, LEAGUES,

AND KINGS

$\mathcal{T}$he period from the death of Alexander the Great of Macedon in 323 to the year 30, when Egypt, the last of the successor kingdoms, fell to Rome, forms an obvious unity, which since the nineteenth century has been recognized by the label "Hellenistic." Yet this epoch also has its own marked phases and interruptions. It reached stable form only about fifty years after Alexander's death, with the definitive establishment of the three great kingdoms of Syria, Egypt, and Macedon. Toward the end of the century, Rome's growing involvement in the affairs of Greece and the eastern Mediterranean created a crisis for the Greek cities, marked by a flurry of negotiations and appeals. Thereafter the Hellenistic period may be said to enter on a new phase, in which relations between states were irrevocably altered by a new configuration of powers.[1]

Despite the predominance of the successor kingdoms, and later of Rome, the Greek city was far from extinct as a political unit. Yet for those cities that were not incorporated, with or without their consent, loosely or tightly, in one of the kingdoms, there was often little choice but to enter one of the leagues *(koina)* which are so conspicuous a feature of the history of the third and second centuries. Two are of special importance, the Aetolian and the Achaean. The first, with its heartland to the northwest of the Corinthian Gulf, came during the third century to extend its power over much of central Greece and into the Aegean. For the whole of the century it dominated Delphi and its administrative council, and drew special prestige from having saved the shrine from the Celts in 279/8. The Achaean League, though it did not succeed in extending its power outside the Peloponnese, nevertheless played an essential role in the affairs of Greece; its conflict with the Romans, ending in the Achaean War of 149–146, confirmed Greece as a dependency of Rome. A partial exception to this general dependence or absorption was the island republic of Rhodes. Formed in 408 by a federation (*synoikismos*) of the three existing cities of the island, Lindus, Ialysus, and Camirus, Rhodes by its stable constitution and its commercial success grew into a considerable power, impeccably Hellenic in its pedigree and policy.

All these political units, whatever their size and importance, used Greek as their language of communication and culture. Since all the kings, moreover, considered themselves at least part Greek, with Greek gods and heroes among their ancestors, "Hellas" now designated not only those areas where Greek was spoken by the majority, but also the colonies created by the kings, above all the Seleucids, in their territories. Even so distant a foundation as "Antioch in Persis," the modern Bushire on the Persian Gulf, claimed to be as much a part of "Hellas" as any city in Asia Minor or old Greece, as emerges from its response to a diplomatic request from Magnesia on the Maeander.[2]

This sense of community was reinforced by religion and the worship of shared gods, and the oracular prestige of Apollo of Delphi was still supreme. Thus about 219 the island city of Paros in the Cyclades received a request for help from its colony of Pharos in Dalmatia; though it felt bound to consent as Pharos' "mother city," it first consulted Delphic Apollo.[3] Magnesia on the Maeander did the same before launching a campaign for acknowledgment of its inviolability.[4]

Under these circumstances—the ceaseless mutability of power and influence, set against the seeming permanence of language and cult—the diplomacy of kinship, like diplomacy in general, became more frequent and more complex.[5] To existing webs of relationship, such as that joining Athens with her mythic and historic colonies, were added new ones. Colonizing kings like the early Seleucids called on old Greek cities within their sphere of influence to add settlers to their foundations, for such leavening gave a tinge of Hellenism to new cities in the interior of Asia Minor or in central Asia. Cities with a long record of colonization burnished their links with their daughter cities, as Miletus did with Istria at the mouth of the Danube and with Apollonia in Mysia.[6] There was thus a traffic in kinships at every diplomatic level, reflected also in literature and the arts. Court poets celebrated the divine ancestry of their royal patrons; thus Theocritus sees Ptolemy I, father of the reigning Ptolemy Philadelphus, enthroned on Olympus as a descendant of Heracles.[7]

As was to be expected, a major concern of the diplomacy of kinship, especially in the unstable circumstances of the third century, was that of "assistance" *(boētheia, epikouria)*, sometimes expressed as "forethought" *(pronoia)*. These requests reflect the sleepless need for protection from attack by land or sea, for funds to repair walls and buildings, for an end to quarrels with neighbors or to internal discord. Diplomacy now becomes more elaborate. Embassies are accompanied by a secretary *(grammateus)*, sometimes also by a military escort. They may carry not only diplomatic instruments such as the texts of decrees, but also works of literature in verse or prose to bolster their claims, blurring the line between ambassador and traveling lecturer.

The "help" which cities request of one another or of higher powers can take many forms, but is almost always connected with the fight for survival. As early as the 360s, the new foundation of Megalopolis appealed to its "kin" in Asia for assistance to build its walls. A similar request is the subject of one of the first true documents of kinship diplomacy, a decree of Argos in honor of Rhodes, perhaps from the late fourth century.[8] It begins:

As kinsmen [*syngeneis*] of the Argives, the Rhodians remain good and true friends of the Argive people and of the Greeks in general, and offer every service on land and sea; and when the Argive people sent an embassy to the Rhodians, the latter lent them a hundred talents free of interest both for the repair of the walls and to bring the cavalry up to strength; and after waiting a long time, and seeing the difficulties of our city, [the Rhodians] have now sent an embassy . . . to affirm that the Rhodian people have remained well disposed to the Argive people in the past, and will continue to do so in the future as well.

The Dorian character of Rhodes is already implied in the Homeric Catalogue of Ships, in which the Rhodians are led by a son of Heracles, Tlepolemus, and authors of the fifth century such as Pindar take it for granted.[9] Since the political setting of the document is unknown, it is impossible to measure how much the Rhodians were moved by the mythic link as against other considerations, but there is no reason to suppose, any more than with the loan of the Magnesians to Megalopolis, that it served merely as a diplomatic excuse.

Kinship could also be used to extend another kind of help— diplomatic intervention with a third party. A remarkable example, perhaps of the later third century, concerns a delegation from the city of Heraclea by Mount Latmus in Caria to the Aetolian League. The embassy "renewed the kinship" with the Aetolians, who gave the Heracleans membership in their league and promised to help them on any diplomatic mission they undertook to a King Ptolemy.[10] This kinship originated from the myth of Endymion, which appears to have existed in two forms, a Greek and an Asian one, which gradually coalesced. In its Asian form, Endymion was a simple shepherd with whom the moon goddess fell in love, but in the composite version he was a "wandering hero." Starting from Elis in the Peloponnese, he crossed with his followers to Asia and founded Heraclea, where the formidable Mount Latmus, which dominates the city, became the scene of his affair with the goddess. Before leaving Elis, Endymion fathered a son, Aetolus, who grew up to become the eponymous hero of the Aetolians.[11]

Myth similarly underlies, or at least serves to justify, a diplomatic intervention of Rhodes on behalf of Iasus in Caria. Iasus had its own legend of descent from Argos, since the name Iasus was shared by a mythical king of Argos and by the eponymous founder of the Carian city.[12] The city's advantageous situation and harbor made it an inevitable focus of Rhodian interest, and a series of documents dated from 220 to 214 shows the larger city intervening to protect the smaller against the power of Olympichus, a dynast based at Alinda in northern Caria. Working through a subordinate named Podilus, he had begun to ravage the territory of Iasus, which then called on the Rhodians as "kinsmen and friends." The Rhodians duly passed a decree of their own, in which they declared their determination to maintain the kinship and to protect their kinsmen. They further instructed an embassy to go to Iasus, "renew" the kinship, and make clear their readiness "not to fail the Iasians in any of their interests." In addition, they sent an embassy to Philip V of Macedon as Olympichus' overlord. From the elaborate recording of all these transactions on stone, and the prominence given to the subject of mythic kinship, it may be inferred that the Rhodians successfully used this claim in order to make Podilus retreat. Although their underlying motive was to affirm their own power on the Asian coast, kinship served as a diplomatic pretext not to "stand idly by."[13]

A similar diplomatic maneuver involving Rhodes and Iasus occurred some thirty years later, under very different circumstances. Now the aggressor was the Syrian king Antiochus III, who had garrisoned Iasus as the Romans and their allies moved southward from the Hellespont, bringing in their train pro-Roman refugees from the city. The Roman forces began to ravage the city's territory, as Olympichus had done before. The exiles appealed to the Rhodians, faithful allies of Rome, and urged them "not to allow a kindred city to perish." The Rhodians then induced the Romans to lift the siege.[14]

Another form of "help" in which appeals to kinship could be used, illustrated by the case of the Iasians, is the sheltering of refugees. In the fifth century, Herodotus knew a myth that the Spartans had helped the Minyans exiled from Lemnos, regarding them, like themselves, as descendants of the Argonauts. According to a later tradition, perhaps equally fanciful, the citizens of Trapezus on the Black Sea sheltered their Arcadian kinsmen who refused to be incorporated into Megalopolis. From the third century on, such appeals are well attested. In the year 234 Miletus was asked by Cretan mercenaries, who had served the city and did not wish to return home, to give them sanctuary. The citizens referred the request to their local Apollo, who advised them to grant it. A few years later they passed a decree justifying their earlier decision "by the familiarity and kinship, going back to the god [Apollo], and by the alliance, which the people have observed from their ancestors' time . . . as was fitting since the origin of the kinship goes back to the god."[15] There are several versions of the myth joining Miletus with Crete, but the one followed by the Milesians here may well be one propagated by the Ionian poet Nicander of Colophon. The parents of the eponymous founder, the hero Miletus, were Apollo and a daughter of King Minos. Persecuted by the king (as Bellerophon is persecuted by the king of Argos in Homer), he became a "wandering hero" and settled a new city on the Asian mainland.[16] Whatever the version followed by the Milesians, they took it seriously enough to consult their principal divinity, and to set up a record of these transactions in his chief urban sanctuary, the Delphinion. Nor was the mythical link a mere cover for self-interest, for the inclusion of the Cretans in the Milesian polity was a hazardous step, and as ancestor of both parties the god was both a promoter and a guarantor of its success.

A sign of the social tensions in Hellenistic cities is their frequent recourse to "summoned judges" *(metapemptoi dikastai)*.[17] From the late fourth century on, cities unable to settle their lawsuits internally would call in one or more men from another city, sometimes from several, and this panel would then try the cases brought before it or settle them out of court. The two hundred or more inscriptions which concern such judges also supply more documents of diplomatic kinship than any other class of text, about forty or fifty. This proportion of four to one suggests that, for the largely secular purpose of settling lawsuits and maintaining concord among citizens, it was more important to find judges of known experience and fairness than to seek out kin.[18]

An abiding concern of cities of the third and later centuries, and a subject often mentioned in texts of kinship diplomacy, was that of securing inviolability *(asylia)* for themselves and their sanctuaries, which were often situated outside the city walls, and sometimes several hours' journey away. These appeals rested not only on the inherited sanctity of such sites, but also on a concept deeply embedded in Greek diplomatic practice, that of *sylia,* which can be roughly understood as "the right of seizure or reprisal." From archaic times, cities and individuals exercised the right to seize the goods of persons or corporate entities as reprisal for an alleged wrong. (Herodotus in the opening pages of his *Histories* represents the hostilities between Greeks and barbarians as beginning with just such a series of reprisals, started by the kidnapping of the Argive heroine Io.) This "right of seizure" could be suspended by law or treaty. Thus as early as the sixth century a community of eastern Locrians declared "immune from seizure" *(asylos)* anybody planting land in newly settled territory.[19] From the early third century cities began to take their own initiatives, sending out teams of sacred ambassadors *(theōroi)* in order to request a waiver of the right of seizure, expressed as "inviolability" *(asylia),* the beneficiary being a notable sanctuary or a contest which the city was establishing or enlarging in honor of its patron divinity. Since the prestige of the sanctuary or the contest could not be maintained except by attracting visitors from outside, these requests involved the immunity not only of the sanctuary or the city, but also of those traveling to it; hence the frequency of appeals to notoriously predatory states such as the cities of Crete.[20]

The chronology of several of these appeals is uncertain, being often dependent on criteria such as the paleography of inscriptions. The earliest known is usually taken to be from the island of Tenos in the Cyclades, which began in the 270s or 260s to collect financial contributions and recognition for its new temple of Poseidon. The first reply is from the federal league of Phocis in central Greece, but this uses only the word "familiarity" *(oikeiotēs)*, thus leaving the nature of the link undefined. A large number of replies from cities of Crete "renew" an earlier accord, and these probably belong to the early second century. One at least talks of the Tenians as "kindred" *(syngeneis)*, so that Tenos must have appealed to such a link in its original campaign, and the tie is doubtless King Minos' legendary naval empire. The renewal of the plea suggests that it had come to lose its force in the last years of the century, that troubled period in which the international conflicts taking place in the eastern Mediterranean had reopened the seas to piracy.[21]

About the same time as Tenos, another island city, Cos, began to collect similar acknowledgments from friendly kings on behalf of its renowned medical sanctuary of Asclepius.[22] In 242 the city expanded its claim and began to seek recognition of its contest in honor of the god, which it now proposed to hold on a four-year cycle like the great contests of Greece, the Olympia and the Pythia, though as yet there was no talk of immunity for the city itself or its territory. Its ambassadors appealed to the Hellenism of kings and other cities, and wherever possible to their kinship. A revealing reply is from the ruler of a half-Greek kingdom which can only be the Cimmerian Bosporus, the modern Kertsch in the Crimea. This had long been known to the Mediterranean Greeks as a source of wheat, and in the first half of the third century had reached unprecedented levels of prosperity. The writer "accepts with pleasure the kinship as true and worthy both of you and of us," and complains mildly that other Greeks have been slow to acknowledge the relationship. He is perhaps thinking above all of Athens, which had not gone further than to honor his predecessor Spartocus as "familiar" *(oikeios)*.[23]

No doubt the Cretan cities would have been high on the Coans' visiting list, but no replies from them have been published.

Two Sicilian cities, Camarina and Gela, speak warmly of their kinship with Cos, claiming always to reaffirm it when they make their ancestral sacrifices. This link was created less than a hundred years before, when many cities of Sicily were refounded by the Corinthian Timoleon.[24] The fact that such a recent event could be placed on a level with mythic ones is yet another sign that the distinction between myth and history was only one of distance in time.

Several Macedonian cities, prompted by their king Antigonus Gonatas, accept the Coans' immunity, but speak only of "familiarity" *(oikeiotēs)* with them, not kinship. In this case, as with the Athenians and King Spartocus, the term appears designed to underline the absence of kinship, perhaps because Antigonus did not wish to make an outright acknowledgment of the Coans' request.[25]

No less than three requests for immunity, but this time involving cities and their territory, and not merely their dependent sanctuaries, appear within a short space of time from about 208 to 203 (though the dating of one is controversial). All the cities involved are in the southwest of the Asian peninsula: Magnesia on the Maeander, Teos, and Alabanda. The concentration of these diplomatic campaigns within so short a period demands an explanation, and it is to be sought in political developments on the Greek mainland and in Asia. In Greece, the war between Rome and its allies against Philip V of Macedon began to falter in 208, when Attalus of Pergamum, one of the principal Roman allies, was forced to return home. For two years Rome neglected the war, and in 206 its other chief ally, Aetolia, signed a separate peace with Philip. A general peace, not destined to last, was signed late in October of the next year at Phoenice in Epirus. At the same moment, Antiochus III of Syria was returning from his expedition into the eastern satrapies of the kingdom, his "march up-country" *(anabasis)*. Within a short time both Antiochus and Philip, whose hands had been freed by the peace of 205, were to make their appearance in this same corner of Asia Minor. It was a crucial moment, in which a successful claim for immunity might save a city from pillage or destruction.[26]

The Magnesians' campaign is the earliest of the three, and concerns the contest celebrated by the city in honor of its local goddess, Artemis "of the White Cliff" *(Leucophryēnē)*. After an earlier attempt to raise the status of the Leucophryena by granting money prizes, in 208 the Magnesians decided to elevate it to full international rank by issuing prizes consisting only of crowns, as in the great games of Greece. Their sacred ambassadors fanned out carrying two documents, both of which laid especial emphasis on the city's links with Crete—a brief history of the original founders' migration from Magnesia in Thessaly to Crete and then to Asia, and a decree of the prehistoric Cretans wishing them success.[27]

Of the sixty or so respondents, only a fraction mention kinship with Magnesia, though there are certainly "kindred" states among the others. In some cases the link is mythical, as with certain cities of Thessaly and with one which is probably to be identified with Mytilene, since a legendary king of Lesbos, Macar, was the brother of Magnes, the eponym of the Magnesians. A response from the city of Same on Cephallenia illustrates the elaborate care with which such claims might be advanced. Here the Magnesian ambassadors cite "oracles, poets, and honorable decrees from various cities . . . and discourse on the familiarity [*oikeiotēs*] that exists between [the two cities] because of the kinship [*syngeneia*] of Magnes and Cephalus, son of Deion." The Cephallenians grant all the ambassadors' requests and invite them to the local contest in honor of their eponym Cephalus.[28] In myth, Deion and Magnes were among the seven sons of Aeolus, the ancestor of the Aeolians. The poets cited by the Magnesians no doubt related exploits from the city's heroic past, while in return the Cephallenians invited them to the festival of their own founder.

In other cases, however, the link was more recent. Several generations before, Magnesia had been requested by the Seleucid king Antiochus I to supply colonists for his settlements in western and central Asia. It thus became, in effect, an artificial mother city of the new foundations, which in the traditional way inherited the ties and traditions of their parent.[29] The best preserved of these replies is from the city of Antioch in Persis, where Antiochus III was staying at this very time.[30] The citizens praise the Magnesian ambassadors for recalling the kinship between their two cities; they declare their own reverence for the gods whom both cities worship in common; and they pray for Magnesians to persevere in their present political conduct. This last is a diplomatic hint at their loyalty to the Seleucids, a crucial issue in these years when war was impending in western Asia.

The political background implied in the campaign of Magnesia is more explicit in the case of Teos. On the usual reconstruction of the chronology, Antiochus III, having recently returned from his march up-country, made a foray into the eastern Aegean in 204 or 203. In the course of this he seized the port city of Teos, which was well positioned for threatening the other Ionian cities, and yet vulnerable to attack by sea.[31] The king now appeared before the Teians to declare both city and territory "sacred and immune from seizure" *(hiera kai asylos)*. Like the Magnesians, the Teians began a campaign to have this status internationally recognized. Most of the replies come from cities of Crete, of which many declare the Teians "kinsmen," though some call them only "familiar" *(oikeioi)*, a distinction that in this case seems to be of no importance. The link is presumably, as in the case of Cos, that of the ancient Minoan thalassocracy. Both Antiochus III and Philip V sent their own representatives to accompany the ambassadors in Crete, a sign of the importance that they attached to the success of the mission. Teos' geographical position made it easy prey for pirates, and this danger must have contributed to the urgency of its quest for inviolability.[32]

At almost the same time, Alabanda in Caria, which around the middle of the century had been refounded as Antioch of the Chrysaorians, started a similar campaign under circumstances very similar to those of Teos. Again backed by their "benefactor" Antiochus III, the Alabandans sought to put their whole city and territory under the protection of two local gods, Zeus of the Chrysaorians and Apollo Isotimus. Of the two replies that are preserved, one from Athens makes no mention of kinship, which the Athenians were always reluctant to acknowledge with other peoples. The Delphians use an expression of unusual vagueness, calling the Alabandans "kin to the Greeks" *(syngenēs tōn Hellēnōn)*.[33] The reason is probably not disdain of Alabanda as a latecomer to Hellenism, but on the contrary its position as a leading city of the "Chrysaorian league," a confederation of Carian cities which took its name from the hero Chrysaor.[34] He in turn was of the line of Bellerophon, the "wandering hero" from Ephyre in the Argolid.

Chrysaor recurs in a text of exactly this same period, the longest and most elaborate document of kinship diplomacy that has survived on stone, though it does not involve immunity, but rather a loan for the rebuilding of walls.[35] The text was set up by the city of Xanthus in Lycia, on a great stele erected in its sanctuary of Leto. In the year 206/5 the Xanthians received an embassy from Cytenion, the federal center of the "Dorians of the Metropolis." Some twenty years before, Cytenion had been devastated by an earthquake and its walls demolished, and this misfortune had tempted the then king of Macedonia, Antigonus Doson, to invade the region. The Aetolians, to whose league the Cytenians belonged, had just signed a separate peace with the current king of Macedon, Philip V, and, no doubt concerned for their own and their allies' security, they encouraged the Cytenians to seek funds for the purpose of repairing their walls. When the ambassadors reached Xanthus, they were on their way to two eastern kings, Antiochus III of Syria and Ptolemy IV of Egypt, both of whom claimed descent from Heracles, the especial hero of the Dorians. Though the Xanthians were able to make a gift of only five hundred drachmai (about two kilograms of silver), far less than what the Magnesians had given to Megalopolis in 370, they recorded the transaction in detail, including the mythological arguments of the Cytenians:

> They request us, recalling the kinship that exists between them and us from gods and heroes, not to allow the walls of their city to remain demolished. Leto [they say], the goddess who presides over our city [*archēgetis*], gave birth to Artemis

and Apollo amongst us; from Apollo and Coronis the daughter of Phlegyas, who was descended from Dorus, Asclepius was born in Doris [that is, the land of the Dorians]. In addition to the kinship that exists between them and us (deriving) from these gods, they also recounted the bond of kinship [*symplokē tou genous*] which exists between us (deriving) from the heroes, presenting the genealogy between Aiolus and Dorus. As well, they indicated that the colonists sent out from our land by Chrysaor, the son of Glaucus, the son of Hippolochus, received protection from Aletes, one of the descendants of Heracles: for [Aletes], starting from Doris, came to their aid when they were being warred upon. Putting an end to the danger by which they were beset, he married the daughter of Aor, the son of Chrysaor. Indicating by many other proofs the goodwill that they had customarily felt for us from ancient times because of the tie of kinship, they asked us not to allow the greatest of the cities of the Metropolis to be obliterated.[36]

In this elaborate mythical scheme, a number of strands come together. Chrysaor is a descendant of the Homeric Glaucus, and thus of the famous Bellerophon, but he is also the eponymous founder of the Chrysaorian league of Caria. At the same time, his son Aor joins forces with Aletes the Heraclid, whose very name means "the wanderer," and who goes on to become the first Dorian king of Corinth. Thus the line of Chrysaor is linked to that of Heracles, and thereafter to kings who claimed descent from him.

If this flurry of diplomatic activity from 208 to 203 reflects fears of renewed war between the great powers, those fears were soon to be justified. Immediately after the peace of Phoenice, Philip V began to extend his power into the Aegean and into the Asian seaboard, and his example was quickly followed by Antiochus III; in the winter of 203/2 the two kings made a secret pact to divide up the overseas possessions of Egypt; in 200 the Roman people, recently released from their war with Carthage, voted to renew war with Philip; and within a few years Rome was embroiled, first in unfriendly negotiations and finally in war, with Antiochus. From this point on the spread of Roman power in the East can be measured in a series of milestones, beginning with the defeats of Philip at Cynoscephalae in 197, of Antiochus III at Magnesia in 190, of Philip's son Perseus at Pydna in 168, and finally of Antony and Cleopatra, and with them the last successor kingdom, in 30. Long before that date, however, Rome had established direct or indirect rule over most of the Greek-speaking world, or held so strong a position in relation to local kings as effectively to direct their policies. One major interruption in this process was provided by a kingdom which came into prominence only in the second century, that of the Pontic kings, with their capital at Sinope on the Black Sea. The last of these, Mithridates VI, was to bring much of Asia Minor and Greece to his side in a great war with Rome fought in the years 88–84.

The Romans represented a new kind of power, no less pious and no less sensitive to claims of kinship, but with different traditions of war and peace, diplomacy and religion. The propaganda of Pyrrhus of Epirus showed that the legend of Rome's founding by the Trojan Aeneas had long been familiar to the Greeks, and it will be seen later how Rome turned this legend to its own advantage, presenting itself not as an enemy but precisely as savior and friend, first of the western Greeks and then of their cousins in old Greece and in the east. Thus the entry of Rome into the eastern theater, so far from bringing an end to appeals based on Greek myth and history, gave them new currency. On the one hand, alert Greek communities were quick to exploit the advantages to be gained from kinship with the new power. The outstanding example is Ilium, the successor city to Homeric Troy. But even among cities not linked to Rome by kinship, some of them in still independent kingdoms, such diplomacy continued as actively as before, but with a perceptible change. Appeals for diplomatic, military, and financial help largely ceased. Instead there began a process, which was to be much more marked in the imperial period, whereby communities looked to their divine and heroic past for affirmation of their prestige. Diplomacy now took on a cere-monial aspect, which it is easy to mistake for futile nostalgia. In fact, tradition and religion served to mark a city's status in relation to other ones near and far, and sometimes to impress the Roman power with the city's antiquity and its worth as a possible recipi-ent of benefits.

A typical document of this new atmosphere is from Miletus in Ionia. At some time in the second century, this ancient city, proud of its tradition of foundation from Crete and its own long record of colonization, received an embassy from the city of Apollonia in Mysia. This had been founded by Miletus in the ar-chaic period, but the connection had evidently weakened over time. The Milesians duly listened to the ambassadors, inspected the documents they had brought, and concluded that their own ancestors had indeed colonized Apollonia, driving out the barbar-ians who had previously inhabited the land. They accordingly permitted the Apolloniates to set up a permanent memorial of this transaction in the Delphinion, the same sanctuary in which they themselves had recorded their own grant of citizenship to Cretan mercenaries.[37] This outspoken Hellenism was a portent of the fu-ture, when Miletus would incorporate its colonizing past into its official titulature, calling itself "mother city of many great cities in the Pontus, in Egypt, and in many parts of the world."[38]

Another such portent is the representation of kindred or allied cities in works of art. The sanctuary of Hecate at Lagina, a de-pendency of Stratonicea in Caria, carried a frieze on which vari-ous cities of the region appear as personifications carved in high relief. Not all are recognizable, but the joint community of Aphrodisias and Plarasa, formed with Roman encouragement probably in the mid-second century, can be made out, as can its neighbor Gordiouteichos, with its eponymous hero Gordius rep-resented as a helmeted warrior. The frieze must represent some grouping of Carian cities, probably not the so-called Chrysaorian league but one centered on the cult of Hecate. The inclusion of Aphrodisias points to Roman influence on the league's member-ship.[39]

This fabric of kinship and interconnectedness, fostered by Roman power, was to be rudely though not irreparably torn by the incursion of Mithridates of Pontus in the 80s. Mithridates' predecessors, notably his father, Mithridates V, had already advertised their goodwill toward the Greeks in the previous century, above all by benefactions to the city that stood as the embodiment of Hellenic culture, Athens. The king now played on Greek sentiment by appealing to his connection with Greek gods and heroes. On his coins he displayed a latecomer to Olympus, the semi-heroic Dionysus, whose name he later placed among his own titles, perhaps recalling the god as an eastern conqueror who brought the Greek world under his benign sway. On other coins Mithridates used the hero Perseus as an emblem. Perseus was both Greek by origin and the eponymous hero of the Persians, to whom Mithridates was related by his Iranian descent. The king's motive in using him is thus an echo, whether conscious or not, of the appeal which Herodotus attributes to Xerxes on the eve of his invasion of Greece. It was a major coup when, despite this Iranian connection, Mithridates won the support of Athens; conceivably his spokesmen reminded the Athenians that their goddess had helped Perseus in his struggle with the monstrous Gorgon.[40]

For Mithridates, any disadvantage that might appear to flow from recalling his Iranian heritage was outweighed by the appeal to Greek gods and heroes. The Greeks were far from thinking that their gods belonged to them alone, least of all Zeus, the father of gods and men, whose protection of family ties and guest-friends applied throughout the world. He could be recognized under the mask of the supreme god of barbarians such as the Persians or (when they became known to the Greeks) the Jews.

At the same time, the attraction of Greek culture, so powerfully illustrated by the philhellenism of foreign potentates such as Croesus and Amasis in the sixth century, Alexander I of Macedon in the fifth, and the unnamed king of the Cimmerian Bosporus in the third, also magnetized states whose claims to Greekness were at the best indirect. Two such, the Lycians and the Jews, form a transition to the most important of such states, Rome.

6

LYCIANS AND JEWS

$\mathscr{T}$he Lycians and the Jews, two peoples unconnected with each other and each in their own way united by tradition and culture, form an instructive contrast in kinship diplomacy. The Lycians had long since gained a place in Greek consciousness by their inclusion in the *Iliad,* which served the Greeks as their national epic. The Jews were comparative latecomers, but no laggards in their use of Greek thought and diplomatic forms.

In Homer, the Lycians are steadfast allies of the Trojans, and their leader, Sarpedon, is second only to Hector among the enemies of the Greeks. At the same time, Sarpedon and his cousin Glaucus are linked to Greece by descent, since their ancestor Bellerophon comes from "Ephyre in a corner of horse-breeding Argos."[1] The poet does not explain or motivate the alliance between Trojans and Lycians, and, as we have seen, the whole episode may have been grafted on to the poem in the sixth century, when the culture of Lycia started to acquire a strongly Greek character. Striking testimony to this Hellenization comes from a tomb in central Lycia which displays various scenes of Greek mythology on its walls, among them the birth of Bellerophon's horse, Pegasus, and of its twin, the giant Chrysaor.[2] As early as the eighth century the city of Corinth, a flourishing center of commerce in the archaic period, had appropriated the traditions of Ephyre, identifying a celebrated spring outside the city as the place of Pegasus' miraculous birth.[3]

The antiquities, real or imagined, of Lycia, soon attracted Greek inquiry and speculation. A striking departure from the Homeric version made Sarpedon not a prince born in Lycia, but a brother of Minos who had emigrated from Crete to the mainland. Herodotus accepts this version, and combines it with another that traced the Lycians back to Lycus, a son of King Pandion of Athens.[4] Herodotus' fellow citizen Panyassis, an epic poet writing in the first half of the fifth century, introduced Lycia into his poem on the deeds of Heracles, narrating how the hero defeated Tlous, Pinarus, and Cragus, the three sons of "the great Termiles." The sons' names show them to be eponyms of cities in the region of Xanthus, Tlos, Pinara, and Cragus, just as their father's name makes him the eponymous ancestor of the "Tremileis," the name of the Lycians in their own language. Though Panyassis is using traditional motifs of kinship, especially the motif of the three eponymous brothers, such detailed knowledge must be drawn from local sources.[5]

In due course Lycia began to produce its own local historians, of whom one, a certain Menecrates, wrote not later than the second century. A fragment is preserved by a Greek historian of Rome, Dionysius of Halicarnassus (the third author from this city to enter into the traditions of Lycia), and it suggests how such historians used older elements to create new links. In the *Iliad,* the hero Aeneas, son of Anchises and Aphrodite, is associated with the Lycian Pandarus, who in historical times received heroic honors at Pinara.[6] Moreover, the god Poseidon forecasts that Aeneas and his descendants will one day rule over the Trojans, a prophecy which has often been thought to reflect the claims of some principality in the Troad or elsewhere in the archaic age.[7] These two elements, the connection of Aeneas with Pandarus and the promise of his future rule, help explain a story which Menecrates either devised by himself or adapted from a predecessor. According to this, Aeneas betrayed Troy to the Achaeans after quarreling with Paris (Alexander). He thus survived the fall of the city and became an Achaean (we do not know whether in this version he remained in the Troad).[8] This is not the only genealogical reconstruction to be based on Poseidon's prophecy, since it also contributed to the much more enduring belief that Aeneas, after sailing to the west, founded a new kingdom in Sicily or Italy. But it is probably this mythological link that underlies the long tradition, first attested in the Hellenistic period, of a special relationship between Lycia and Rome.[9]

Whereas for Homer Xanthus was only a river, named for its yellow color *(xanthos),* by the fifth century there had grown up near the mouth of the river a city of the same name which was to remain the capital of the Lycian federation. It owed its prestige in part to its sanctuary of a mother goddess who became identified with Leto, the mother of Apollo and Artemis. Modern excavation of this site has transformed knowledge of the city as the political and religious center of the Lycians. One discovery there has already been mentioned, an enormous stele commemorating an appeal to the Xanthians by the Dorians of the Metropolis, the same region which Sparta had gone to help in the 450s. In order to raise money for the rebuilding of their walls, the Cytenian ambassadors visited Xanthus in 205 and recited a long mythological tale, involving both gods and heroes, with the clear intention of linking their homeland with the Lycians.

The heart of their account is, once again, the forerunner of all these myths of kinship, the speech of Glaucus the Lycian in the sixth book of the Iliad. The hero there traced his own ancestry back to Bellerophon, the exile from the Argolid who came to the "swift-eddying Xanthus," married the local king's daughter, and founded a line of rulers. The ambassadors now take the story further. The Homeric Glaucus was succeeded as ruler of Xanthus by his son Chrysaor, who sent his own son, named Aor, to lead a group of colonists back to Greece. These settled somewhere in the region of Mount Parnassus, and helped the descendants of Heracles in their campaign to win back their rightful heritage in the Peloponnese. As part of these adventures, Aor married the daughter of the Heraclid Aletes (the familiar motif of the king's daughter) and helped to establish him as the first Dorian king of Corinth. The ambassadors cunningly closed the circle of myth with this device, making a descendant of Bellerophon return to the very city from which his ancestor had been unjustly driven out, that is, Ephyre, now renamed Corinth. Chrysaor is no longer the monstrous twin of Pegasus, but a Lycian prince who in traditional fashion sends colonists out to faraway lands, conveniently creating opportunities for future diplomats. Among the cities which the Dorian ambassadors had already visited were doubtless those of the Chrysaorian league of Caria, which claimed its own links with Bellerophon and Pegasus.[10]

The outbreak of war between Rome and Philip, five years after the visit of the Dorians to Xanthus, was heavy with consequences for most of the Greek world, to which Lycia now firmly belonged. One such consequence was the decision of Antiochus III to reclaim his ancestral possessions in southern and western Asia Minor, and to place his eldest son on the throne of Thrace, an undertaking which led inexorably to conflict with Rome and to his own defeat at Magnesia in the year 190. An inscription from the city gate of Xanthus commemorates the king's passage through Lycia in 197, and is still visible despite a halfhearted attempt to erase it: "The Great King Antiochus sanctified the city to Leto, Apollo, and Artemis because of the kinship which connected him with them." Whether the city had resisted the king in his advance, and exactly what his "sanctification" of it implies, are unclear, but it must have escaped heavy damage and the quartering of unfriendly troops thanks to an act of the king, who like all the Seleucids claimed descent from the god Apollo.[11] No doubt the citizens had reminded the king or one of his generals of the importance of their sanctuary of Leto, where the goddess was believed to have given birth to her divine twins, just as the citizens of Mallus in Cilicia reminded Alexander of their foundation by Heracles.

It so happens that an inscription from the Letoon, dated to the very next year, also refers to a mythic relationship of Xanthus, but one involving a completely different lineage. The city of Ilium inherited one of the names, and all the prestige, of the Homeric Troy, and turned its mythic past to profit under Alexander and the Seleucids, who during the first part of the third century were a major presence in western Asia.[12] When Antiochus was in western Asia and had already recovered Ilium, a certain Themistocles, a citizen of Ilium and a public speaker *(rhētōr),* visited Xanthus. There he gave displays of his art, "staying no short time in our city, and proving himself unexceptionable and worthy of the kinship that links us with the Ilians."[13] Themistocles must have used his lectures to illustrate the hereditary links between the two cities, and thus to fill in a blank left by Homer, the motivation for the Lycians' presence at the side of the Trojans. Such was the ingenuity which went into this type of demonstration—for example, the link between the Armenians and the Thessalians, or the elaborate tale which the Dorian ambassadors had spun in Xanthus only a few years before—that his precise arguments must remain beyond recovery. It is clear, nonetheless, that behind the visit of Themistocles and his mythological lectures there lies a contemporary reality—the renewed Seleucid presence in Asia Minor.

After the Roman defeat of Antiochus at Magnesia, ten commissioners sent out by the senate arrived to settle the affairs of Asia and to reward friends and punish enemies. The Rhodians, who had been among the Romans' staunchest allies, asked to be given control over Lycia and a large part of Caria as their reward, while the Lycians, who had remained true to Antiochus until the end, turned to their kinsmen of Ilium for help. Polybius, who is normally indifferent to such factors, notes that Ilian ambassadors pleaded with the Romans "because of the familiarity [*oikeiotēs*] between them that the Lycians be pardoned for their errors." The Greek is ambiguous, but the natural interpretation is that "familiarity" is being used as a more general term than "kinship," and refers to the Ilians and the Lycians.[14] In any case, the commissioners took no severer measures than to assign Lycia to the Rhodians, but by doing so created a diplomatic contretemps. The Ilians proceeded to inform the Lycians that they had saved them from Rhodian domination, while the Rhodians assumed that they had been given Lycia "as a gift." Some twenty years later, in 167, Rome had just defeated Perseus, the last king of Macedon, and now felt less compunction about imposing its will on the Greek East. Long since jealous of Rhodes, the senate determined that it had not after all given Lycia to the Rhodians, and declared it free.[15]

The Roman liberation of Lycia, however tardy and self-interested, appears to be commemorated in a monument on the Capitol of which fragments still survive. It was inscribed with dedications made by communities and kings of Asia in honor of the Roman people.[16] The date is uncertain, but the original may have been set up in 167, damaged by fire in the civil war of 83, and then reinscribed. In one of the texts carved on the monument, the Lycian league honors the Romans for the restoration of its "democracy," probably an allusion to the liberation of 167. In a second text, the Lycians call the Roman people "kindred, friendly, allied" *(cognatum, amicum, socium).*[17] To inscribe such a text in so official a place, the Lycians must have received permission from the senate, presumably in the form of a solemn "nomination" as "kinsmen, friends, and allies." This practice of "naming" friendly persons or nations is characteristically Roman, and we shall see it applied also to a Gallic tribe, the Aedui, later in the century. In the imperial period, it lives on in the practice of permitting Greek cities to carry titles such as "friend and ally of the Romans" or "familiar friends of the emperors."

After the second century, the kinship between Rome and Lycia disappears from the historical record, though it survives in literature. Just as the Lycians had been prominent in Greece's national epic, so they appear, fleetingly but tellingly, in Rome's. When a storm attacks the fleet of Aeneas in the first book of the *Aeneid,* a conspicuous victim is "one ship, which bore the Lycians and the faithful Orontes." The prominence given to this ship serves to link the Roman poem with the Greek one and also, by the word "faithful" *(fidus),* to recall the mythical kinship between the two peoples.[18] A Greek contemporary of Vergil, the geographer Strabo, notes the stability and prosperity of the Lycians under Roman rule. That record was broken in the reign of Claudius, when their unruliness caused the emperor to take away their liberty and incorporate Lycia as a Roman province. It continued to conduct diplomacy, sometimes invoking the kinship which bound its various cities, and as late as the third century Rome was believed to pay special respect to the high priest of the province, the so-called Lyciarch, "because of their ancient alliance."[19]

A curious illustration of the links between Corinth (now a Roman colony), Lycia, and Rome is found in a collection of documents honoring a wealthy Corinthian woman, Junia Theodora. Besides owning property in Lycia, Theodora undertook to give shelter to certain Lycian exiles, who had perhaps left during the political troubles of Claudius' reign. The sheltering of exiles was a traditional duty of kindred states, and it is a sign of the imperial period that individuals start to assume the responsibilities that were once borne by whole cities.[20]

By contrast with the Lycians, whose political importance faded after the second century, the Jews managed in this same century to establish a political entity in their own land, when they gained their freedom from the conjoint yoke of Seleucids and Ptolemies. The struggle that brought about this event was linked above all with the family of the Maccabees or "Hasmoneans," and in particular with the uprising begun by the patriarch Mattathias about 168 and carried on by his sons. In 152 a claimant to the Seleucid throne, Alexander Balas, recognized one of these sons, Jonathan, as high priest, the first of the Hasmonean line. Nine years later, Jonathan was succeeded by his brother Simon, and under Simon's son John Hyrcanus, the most brilliant of the dynasty, Judaea finally shook off the yoke of Syria. It was to remain free, though precariously so, until the reign of Augustus, when Herod I married a Hasmonean princess and began a new dynasty as a client king of Rome.[21]

Though it is the uprising of the Maccabees, as illustrated by the abundant literature which it engendered, which most clearly illuminates the diplomacy of the Jews in the Hellenistic period, Greek speculation about their origins had begun long before.[22] One of the earliest texts to mention the Jews already represents them as Greek in spirit, if not by blood. Clearchus of Soli, a pupil of Aristotle, introduced his master into one of his literary dialogues, attributing to him an encounter with a Jew in Asia. The Jews were a people living in southern Syria and descended from Indian philosophers called Calanoi, though in Syria they were called Jews *(Ioudaioi)* from the land in which they had settled. Aristotle had heard the Jewish sage, "Hellenic not only in language but also in spirit," engage in erudite discussion with certain Greeks in Asia, and so had been moved to admire the man's "extraordinary endurance and self-control in his way of life."[23]

A Greek whose writings about the Jews were to have an even greater impact was an approximate contemporary of Clearchus, Hecataeus of Abdera.[24] His work *On Egypt* presented Moses in the typically Hellenistic guise of a culture-hero, simultaneously ruler, general, and legislator. When a plague caused the Egyptians to drive all aliens from their land, Moses led his people out of Egypt into Judaea. At the same time, "notable leaders" such as Cadmus and Danaus departed with their followers for Greece.[25] Hecataeus' account is a curious conflation of two traditions. On the Jewish side, he evidently knows of the exodus from Egypt. On the Greek, Danaus like Moses was traditionally regarded as a sojourner in a strange land, since he was Argive by descent, and yet was born in Egypt, from which he returned to Argos and founded the royal line. This line was to produce both Perseus and Heracles.[26]

Besides associating Moses with legendary heroes of Greece, Hecataeus portrayed the Jewish people after their establishment in the Promised Land with features which strongly recall the legend of archaic Sparta:

> The lawgiver laid down many rules about military training, making the young practice courage, endurance, in short bear every kind of hardship. He also led expeditions against the

neighboring tribes and divided the large amount of land he had won into allotments. He gave lots of equal size to ordinary persons, but larger ones to the priests, so that they might enjoy larger incomes, and thus perform the service of god without cessation or distraction. Ordinary people were forbidden to sell their own lots, in case anybody was led by greed to buy lots, oppress the poor, and cause depopulation.[27]

Very little is known about Hecataeus' own career, and we cannot tell whether his ethnographic speculations are linked with contemporary events. It may be relevant that his own city, Abdera, had a rich mythic past, claiming Heracles as its original founder.[28] Hecataeus was a courtier of the first Ptolemy, and is known to have visited Sparta as an ambassador, perhaps in the 290s.[29] Hellenistic ambassadors often disseminated myths of kinship; whether Hecataeus did so on his visit to Sparta is not known, but Alexandria in the early third century, in the first era of scholarship inspired by Alexander's conquests, may well be the setting which generated theories about the place of the Jews in the world of Greek culture.

A later Hellenistic historian, Menander of Ephesus, perhaps writing about 200, appears to have effected a conjunction of another kind between Greek literature and Jewish tradition. In the *Odyssey,* the Spartan king Menelaus tells Telemachus how he wandered for many years after the fall of Troy, visiting among other places Phoenicia and Sidon. Now the first book of Kings represents Solomon in friendly relations with the Sidonian king Hiram. Menander in some way linked the arrival of Menelaus in Phoenicia with the story of Solomon's dealings with Hiram, and local Phoenician historians of unknown date appear to have done the same.[30]

The historiography of the Maccabaean uprising was destined to shape the perception of both earlier and later events, among them the exchanges between Greeks and Jews. Three very dissimilar texts are involved. The so-called First Book of Maccabees, originally written in Hebrew, survives only in a Greek translation which retains many traces of the original language. It covers events from the religious crisis at the beginning of the reign of Antiochus IV to the death of Simon, a period of roughly forty years. Second Maccabees is a condensation of a history written in Greek by one Jason of Cyrene, and covers a much shorter period, from the attempt of Heliodorus, the chancellor of Seleucus IV, to raid the temple chest of Jerusalem to Judas Maccabaeus' victory over the Seleucid general Nicanor in 161. These two books are often dated about 100 before our era, and about two centuries later much of the same material is traversed by the Jewish historian Josephus. He uses First Maccabees, though apparently in a version different from the extant one, but he may not have known Jason or Second Maccabees.[31]

First Maccabees and Josephus attest to diplomacy between high priests of Judaea and the city of Sparta in two different periods. For the first contact, the only source is a letter quoted by both authorities, in a form marked by biblical reminiscences in Maccabees, in a fuller and smoother one by Josephus: while his version does not suffer, as does the one in Maccabees, from having been translated from Greek into Hebrew and back, nonetheless Josephus must have adapted it to fit his own notions of style, and moreover it seems to reproduce a different original, probably from an earlier version of Maccabees than the extant one.[32]

Josephus' version is as follows:

Areus, king of the Lacedaemonians, to Onias, greeting. After reading a certain document, we have found that Jews and Lacedaemonians are of one family [*genos*] and share a connection [*oikeiotēs*] with Abraham. It is therefore just that you as (our) brothers should send to us on any matter you wish. We too will do this, and we shall consider what is yours our own, and will consider you joint owners of what is ours. Demoteles the letter-carrier will transmit [this] letter. The writing is square: the seal is an eagle clutching a serpent.

If the letter is authentic, the writer must be the dynamic Spartan king Areus I, who ruled from 309 to 261, and Onias must be the first high priest of that name, son of Jaddua, who had held office in the time of Alexander III.[33] Whether the letter is genuine, and if not when and by whom it was "forged," have been endlessly debated, and no solution is likely to find universal assent.[34] Much of the debate turns on the "certain document" allegedly read by Areus. The reference to a connection *(oikeiotēs)* with Abraham goes back ultimately to the book of Genesis, with its promise of God to Abraham that "all the nations of the earth will be blessed in [his] seed."[35] The term *oikeiotēs* must here denote some kind of familial relation, and the linking figure may be Heracles, the progenitor of both lines of the Spartan royal house. According to a legend now preserved only by a certain Cleodemus (which need not be the one implied by the letter), Heracles married a granddaughter of Abraham when campaigning against the giant Antaeus in Libya.[36] Another link might have been created out of Menelaus' supposed visit to Phoenicia in the time of Solomon.

In the last analysis, however, the letter must remain under strong suspicion, not so much for details of its content as because of the ancient tendency to fabricate contacts of this kind. An instance again involving relations between the Jews and a foreign power is the *Letter of Aristeas,* allegedly written by a courtier of Ptolemy Philadelphus to describe the translation of the Septuagint into Greek.[37] This includes a friendly exchange between the king and an otherwise known high priest named Eleazar. The king's letter is different in purpose from Areus', but in places remarkably similar in tone. Thus, "you will do us a favor by writing to us on any subject you please, and whatever you wish will be granted as soon as possible."[38] The letter of Areus is perhaps a similar composition of the third or early second century, and as such not essentially different from documents created in a purely Greek environment. A parallel has been drawn with a decree supposedly passed by the united Cretans in mythic times, wishing the Magnesians and their leader Leucippus a safe journey to Asia. This edifying text was used by the Magnesians on the Maeander in their campaign to secure immunity from the Cretans.[39]

Even if the letter of Areus is a Jewish fabrication, the Maccabees need not be the only suspects.[40] A link between Sparta and the Jews, if not explicitly attested earlier, would surely have been welcome to the "Hellenizers," the laxist Jews whom they supplanted. One "Hellenizing" high priest was a certain Jason, who after losing his position set sail for Sparta, expecting, in the words of Second Maccabees, "to receive shelter because of the kinship" between Sparta and the Jews.[41] His successor Menelaus has a "herophoric" name clearly deriving from the Homeric king of Sparta, and such names often denote a claim of civic kinship.[42]

The first of the Maccabees to invoke the link with Sparta is said to be the high priest Jonathan. The letter of Areus discussed above survives as an appendix to a letter which Jonathan is portrayed as writing the Spartan authorities, though the two sources for his letter, First Maccabees and Josephus, give widely divergent texts. In Maccabees, after recalling the letter previously sent by Areus, Jonathan asserts that the Jews "had no need of it, having the holy books in (their) hands." He assures the Spartans that the Jews have never ceased to commemorate them in their sacrifices and prayers, but having now overcome their enemies, they have decided to send ambassadors "to renew the kinship" between the two peoples. In reply, the Spartans pass a decree "concerning alliance and friendship" which is delivered after Jonathan's death to his brother Simon.[43]

By Josephus' account, rather than making an undiplomatic assertion that the Jews had no need of Areus' letter, Jonathan assured them that they had no need of proof *(apodeixis)* of the kinship, since it was confirmed in their sacred scriptures.[44] These "renewals of kinship" often required ambassadors to prove the kinship between the parties. Thus the Dorian ambassadors at Xanthus in Lycia regaled their hosts with a long disquisition on myth, "proving the goodwill that has united our two peoples from early times because of our kinship."[45]

Because no passage in scripture seems to modern eyes to confirm the notion of Jewish kinship with Sparta, this has been thought to confirm the superiority of the version in First

Maccabees. But ancient standards of proof were different, relying on similarity of names, as between Armenus and the Armenians; on similarity of customs, as when Herodotus found traces of Perseus in Egypt; and on other such criteria. In other ways as well, the version in Josephus closely resembles the decrees of Greek cities in the Hellenistic period. Just as the Jews in his version assure the Spartans of their prayers, so the people of Camarina in Sicily, passing a decree of honor of Cos, assert that "we continue to cherish the memory of our kinship with (the Coans) by inviting them and other founders both to our public sacrifices, which we received from them, and to our festivals."[46]

Only Maccabees gives the text of the Spartans' reply, which is addressed not to Jonathan but to his brother Simon. The text of this is unexceptionable, and it is usually considered authentic.[47] Though it does not speak of "kinship" *(syngeneia)* or "familiarity" *(oikeiotēs)* between Spartans and Jews, but only of "friendship" *(philia),* this word by no means excludes a closer relationship. For example, a decree of Gonnoi in Thessaly begins, "Whereas the Magnesians on the Maeander, being friends and kinsmen [*philoi kai syngeneis*] of the Gonneis, have renewed the friendship [*philia*] and familiarity [*oikeiotēs*] which have existed from the earliest times between the Magnesians and the Gonneis . . ."[48]

Both Jonathan's letter, if it is authentic, and the Spartan reply to Simon are connected by First Maccabees with embassies between the Jews and Rome. Rome is a major theme of the Maccabaean chronicler, who prefaces his account of Judas' dealings with Rome with a long and curious disquisition on Roman invincibility.[49] From the early second century, the links between Rome and Sparta were close. Ever since Sparta was forced to join the Achaean League in 192, Spartan exiles had looked to Rome for support; the tensions that developed between Rome and the Achaeans from about 150 gave new hope to enemies of the league, and led eventually to war. After defeating the Achaeans in 146, Rome ordered them to pay Sparta a large indemnity, and exempted the city from the tribute now imposed upon most of Greece.[50] It is not explicitly attested that the Maccabees used their kinship with Sparta to influence Rome, but it is in accordance with Hellenistic practice that ambassadors should appeal on a single mission both to the primary party and to others who might be helpful. As one example, the citizens of Lampsacus in the Hellespont in 196 decided to send ambassadors to their "kinsmen" in Rome, but ordered them to go first to the sister colony of Massilia.[51]

A similar diplomatic démarche on the part of the Maccabees is attested not long afterward in Pergamum. A decree of the city, whose text is given by Josephus, honored Jewish ambassadors as they passed through Pergamum on their return from Rome. Having observed the favorable reception which the Jews had received from the senate, the Pergamenes sent their own embassy to the ruling high priest (probably John Hyrcanus), asking him to "increase and preserve" the friendship between the two peoples. "In the time of Abraham too, the father of all the Jews," they claimed, "our ancestors were friendly to them, as we find in the public records."[52]

While this decree also has been questioned, it too fits into what is known of Hellenistic Pergamum. Like so many cities outside old Greece, Pergamum prided itself on its Heraclid ancestry. According to the local legend, which went back to classical antiquity, the Arcadian princess Auge, after being raped by Heracles, give birth to a hero called Telephus. With her infant son she came to Mysia, and there she married the local king, Teuthras. A decree of Pergamum, perhaps not far in date from the one recorded by Josephus, accords citizenship to the people of Tegea in Arcadia because of their kinship with the Pergamenes. The text is to be entered "in the existing records concerning our kinship with the Tegeates," and is also to be inscribed in a sanctuary which Auge herself had founded in Pergamum.[53] The first of these phrases seems to imply that Pergamum maintained a special archive concerning its kinship with Tegea. When the decree in Josephus refers to "public records" confirming friendship between Pergamum and the Jews, that need not be an invention, and once again the tie probably goes back to the heroic age, whether the link is Heracles, the father of Telephus, or the aftermath of the Trojan War.

Whereas the Lycians had won an early place in Greek myth and literature, as had the Jews' Phoenician cousins, the Jews themselves could be brought into the charmed circle only by speculation and learned theory in the Hellenistic age. The ultimate fates of the two peoples are also far different. Whereas the Lycians ceased to write in their own language after the fourth century,[54] the Jews never abandoned their traditional language and writings. While some, notably the "Hellenizers" overthrown by the Maccabees, made extensive concessions to Greek culture, still their religion or beliefs were not absorbed, as the Lycians' were, in a cosmopolitan Hellenism, though by contrast their offshoot, Christianity, made Hellenism its primary vehicle in its first centuries. Despite these differences, both Lycians and Jews of the second century turned the links forged for them by Greek poets and theorizers to their material advantage. Using the accepted practices of Hellenistic diplomacy, they won favor with the ruling power, which was now no longer Greek but, like themselves, only "akin" to the Greeks. These two peoples thus become a chapter in the story of Rome's acceptance of its own Greek origins—the great triumph of the diplomacy of kinship.

7

THE ROMAN REPUBLIC

*I*n the history of kinship as a bond between states of the Mediterranean, the Romans occupy a special place. Stories of Greek heroes who had wandered to the West—Heracles, Odysseus, Aeneas—can be traced back to the archaic age, and such ideas must have reached Rome at least by the sixth century, when it was still dominated by Etruria. The Roman republic, traditionally supposed to begin in 509, became an ever-growing source of speculation to Greek thinkers as it extended its power over the peninsula, and by the late third century it was enmeshed in a web of myths probably more complicated than any other city of patently non-Greek origin. These myths could sometimes be turned against the Romans, but more often they used them in their own favor, and continued to regulate their conduct by them, not only in the imperial period when their power embraced the whole Mediterranean, but even in the diminished era of Byzantium.

Heracles, the wandering hero par excellence, was probably the first to find a secure foothold in Italy, where he took new forms as the Ercle of the Etruscans, the Hercles or Hercules of the Latins.[1] The poet Stesichorus, active in Sicily or in southern Italy in the early sixth century, places one of the hero's labors, his killing of the monster Geryon, on an island in the Atlantic, and may have brought him back to Greece through Italy.[2] A myth related by Vergil makes the returning hero linger on the site of the future Rome. Here he is entertained by a hero from Arcadia, Evander, who has settled with his followers on the Palatine hill, later the residence of the Caesars. It is uncertain how far back this story goes, but some hints may already have existed in Stesichorus.[3] Roman families such as the Fabii and the Antonii traced their origin back to Heracles and his companions, and the first native historian of Rome, Fabius Pictor writing in the late third century, began his account with the arrival of Heracles in Italy, thus combining family and national history.[4]

The cult of the Dioscuri or "youths of Zeus," the heroes Castor and Pollux, is related to the presence of Heracles in early Roman tradition. The twin brothers are associated with him in myth, since all three sailed together on the *Argo.* They also share with him the status of ancestors of the Spartan royal line, for as their father Tyndareus was a legendary king of Sparta, so Heracles was the ancestor of Aristodemus, whose sons were the first joint kings of Sparta. Like Heracles, the two brothers enjoyed extensive cult in Etruria as well as the Greek cities of Italy, and an inscription discovered at Lavinium shows that they were worshipped by the Latin cities in the sixth or fifth centuries. They miraculously aided the Romans at the battle of Lake Regillus in 499, and were honored with a temple in the Forum.[5]

Though Heracles and Evander were to remain integral to Rome's mythic past, the legend of a Trojan foundation was ultimately to prevail. In the *Iliad,* Aeneas belongs to a cadet branch of the Trojan royal line and, though a loyal warrior for the Trojan cause, is resentful of the line of Priam. As if in compensation, the god Poseidon predicts that he and his descendants will one day rule over the Trojans.[6] The tradition of his arrival in Italy was probably accepted by the Etruscans at a time when they still dominated Rome, to judge by their taste for sixth-century Attic vases showing Aeneas in flight from Troy. By the late fifth century, the historian Hellanicus of Lesbos is cited as saying that Aeneas "came from the Molossians [Epirus] to Italy with Odysseus, and there founded the city, naming it after one of the Trojan women called Rhome."[7] As Greek science advanced, and as antiquarians and others realized that Aeneas' foundation of Rome was irreconcilable with the Romans' own tradition of a founder called Romulus, a version evolved whereby Aeneas had landed in Italy and married the daughter of a local king called Latinus; his son by a Trojan wife, Ascanius, founded Alba Longa near modern Castelgandolfo; and Romulus was born from a woman of the line of Aeneas. As leading families claimed descent from Heracles, so others, the so-called *Troianae gentes,* claimed descent from Aeneas and his companions, and one of these, the Julii, succeeded in imposing a version whereby Ascanius in Italy changed his name to Iulus. Through the account given by Vergil, the accredited bard of Caesar Augustus, this version became canonical, all the more since Augustus' defeated rival, Antony, claimed descent from Heracles and a physical resemblance to his heroic ancestor.[8]

How soon the Greek and Trojan connections of the Romans entered into their dealings with other states cannot be known, but there is an early hint in an incident probably of the 320s. The temptation to represent the Romans as inherently hostile barbarians increased as Roman power spread into southern Italy and came ever closer to the old Greek settlements of Magna Graecia and Sicily. In this process, an essential step was Rome's conquest of the Samnites of the southern Apennines. Probably in the 320s, the city of Tarentum, a colony of Sparta and the leading Greek city of southern Italy, took alarm, and began to assemble a coalition of allies, among them the Samnites. "Some say," reports the geographer Strabo, "that the Laconians joined the Samnites in settling their land, and that is why they are philhellenes and are called 'Pitanatae' [Pitane was a district of Sparta]. But this seems to be a fiction of the Tarentines, who wanted to flatter and at the same time to win over their powerful neighbors; since the Samnites used once upon a time to field eighty thousand infantry and eight thousand horsemen." By appealing to the Samnites as Spartans, the Tarentines were making them "kinsmen" of their own, and representing the Romans, for many decades the scourge of the Samnites, either as outright barbarians or as descendants of Troy.[9]

A few decades later, a similar thrust at Roman barbarism, though this time with an appeal to the Greek traditions of the city, was made by Demetrius Poliorcetes during his brief reign over Macedonia. He is said to have captured pirates operating from Antium, a Roman colony, but to have sent them back to Rome. In so doing, the king cited the kinship of the Greeks and Romans, naturally appealing not to Aeneas but rather to the ancient cult of the Dioscuri. "It was wrong, he said, that those who controlled Italy, and had built a sanctuary of the Dioscuri in their forum, where they worshipped those whom all men called 'Saviors,' at the same time should send people to Greece in order to plunder the heroes' ancestral land. The Romans stopped the Antiates from such practices."[10] This story has been thought fictitious, a rhetorical invention of the Sicilian historian Timaeus, presumably because such arguments seem out of place in diplomacy.[11] Yet it shows exactly the same combination of kinship and religion that is found, for example, in the appeal of the Dorian ambassadors at Xanthus. The king's emphasis on the Greek rather than the Trojan side of Rome's mythical lineage is also in accordance with diplomatic practice. His concern is to appeal to Rome's better instincts, to shame it into civilized behavior, and for this purpose he uses those of its myths which served his purpose.

For the war which grew out of Pyrrhus' two excursions to the West, the struggle between Rome and Carthage more usually called the First Punic War, a new historical source becomes our principal guide, the Achaean Polybius, writing in the later second century. Like Thucydides, Polybius is reluctant to admit supernatural causation into history, though he leaves a large field for a principle which he calls "chance" or "fortune" *(tychē)*. He is also hostile to historians who adorn their works with what he considers trivialities, such as interstate kinships and foundations of cities.[12] Like Thucydides, however, Polybius occasionally allows his historical actors to be influenced by such considerations, and to refer to them in their speeches.

Polybius rightly sees the First Punic War as a war for Sicily, the island which lay as a geographic and economic prize between the two empires.[13] While the Carthaginians had long been established in the western part of the island, and the Greeks in the eastern, the Romans' claim to an interest in its affairs was tenuous, but a lucky chance dealt them a diplomatic card. A tradition already known to Thucydides held that the Trojans who escaped the fall of their city had settled in northwestern Sicily and formed with the local tribe of the Sicani a people called Elymoi.[14] Two cities claimed to owe their foundation to the Elymoi, and both were to play a major role in the propaganda and the fighting of the war. Eryx on the coast had a celebrated sanctuary originally dedicated to the Phoenician Astarte. By a natural process of Greek interpretation, the goddess became Aphrodite, and the founder of the city an eponymous Eryx. This was perhaps enough to justify the belief that Aeneas, the son of Aphrodite, had landed here after his escape from Troy.[15] Inland from Eryx lay the city of Egesta or Segesta, the capital of the Elymoi. Legends which are for us not earlier than the Augustan age trace the city's Trojan origins to a time before the war of Homer's *Iliad,* a device perhaps intended to mark its precedence over other cities of the region.[16] As early as 263, the second year of the war, the Segestans betrayed their Carthaginian garrison and went over to Rome, alleging their kinship with Rome, or so it is asserted by historians later than Polybius. In retaliation, the Carthaginians subjected the Segestans to a bitter siege, which the Romans were able to raise only in 260.[17] The sanctuary of Eryx, however, remained in Carthaginian hands until 249, when it was captured by the Romans. There followed a long and bitter struggle, which Polybius compares to a cockfight in which the adversaries refuse to yield, even with blood pouring from their wounds.[18]

After the end of the war in 241, Rome settled the status of the whole island, except for the part ruled by Hiero of Syracuse, and probably at the same time declared the city of Segesta immune and free.[19] This may well be the occasion of a senatorial decree mentioned by Diodorus of Sicily. After describing the sanctuary and its importance to the Romans, he observes: "The Roman senate, in its eagerness to honor the goddess, decreed that the seventeen cities of Sicily most loyal to Rome should wear gold [*chrysophorein*] in honor of Aphrodite, and that two hundred soldiers should guard the sanctuary."[20] The word *chrysophorein* was long taken to mean "to bring gold" and to refer to the payment of tribute. The actual meaning is "to wear gold," and this gives the key to the decree. Familiar with the device of employing religious leagues as an expression of political control, the Romans now extended the principle to Sicily. The cities most loyal to them were to join in a league in which the goddess, "golden Aphrodite," was to be honored by recurrent festivals. This device not only drew attention to a favorite theme of their own propaganda, "trust" or *fides*. It also made the league of Aphrodite of Eryx the first in a series of religious organizations in which the Romans exploited their own mythic kinship with Aphrodite in order to cement the goodwill of their Greek allies. During the Second Punic War, the Romans established a temple of Venus of Eryx on their own Capitol, and about the year 60 B.C.E. a Roman denarius depicts the original foundation, a temple perched on a rocky summit and surrounded by massive walls (Figure 2).[21]

Thus the First Punic War assured the preponderance of Troy in the mythology of Rome, but by doing so put the Romans at a disadvantage in the following decades, as they were drawn ever more into the affairs of Greece and Macedonia. Two alleged incidents, it is true, appear to show the opposite, but they are probably fictitious. According to the Augustan historian Pompeius Trogus, the Acarnanians of northwestern Greece denounced the Aetolian League to the Roman senate in the early 230s and requested that they themselves should receive Roman help "as the only people which had not aided the Greeks against the Trojans, who were the ancestors of the [Roman] race." The Acarnanians are known to have made a similar plea in the 190s after the defeat of Philip V, when many Greek states had come to see the advan-

Figure 2. Coin of M. Considius Nonianus,
showing temple of Venus at Eryx

tage of appealing to Rome's Trojan ancestry; and Polybius explicitly dates the first Roman "involvement" *(epiplokē)* in eastern
Greek affairs to 228.[22] Blame for the fabrication has been fixed,
with probable justice, on the Roman "annalists." These early Roman historians, beginning with Fabius Pictor in the last quarter of
the third century, were not above stretching the truth in order to
glorify Rome's ancient lineage and hereditary piety.

Similar considerations weigh against what Suetonius reports of
the emperor Claudius and the "Ilians," that is, the citizens of the
Greek city which had succeeded Homeric Troy: "He gave the
Ilians immunity from tribute in perpetuity as ancestors of the Roman people, reading out an ancient letter from the senate and
people of Rome in Greek, whereby they promised friendship and
alliance to King Seleucus if he freed their kinsmen [*consanguinei*]
the Trojans of all obligations." (Seleucus is probably the second
of the name, who reigned from 246 to 226.) This exchange
looks like another retrojection from the 190s, when Rome and
Antiochus III were struggling for control of western Asia Minor,
with Ilium serving as a propaganda trophy much as Segesta and

Eryx had served in the First Punic War. As with the story of the Acarnanians' appeal, it is reasonable to look for the origin in propaganda, which then passed into the work of Roman annalists.[23]

A more plausibly recorded incident of the year 228 shows the Romans' entry into one of the most cherished institutions of Greek culture, interstate athletics. When Roman ambassadors arrived in Corinth, which at that time controlled the Isthmian games, the city used the occasion to admit Roman competitors to the games, and—perhaps by deft arrangement, not unparalleled in international contests today—a Roman called Plautus won the sprint.[24] The meager evidence for this incident does not indicate whether issues of kinship were raised, or quietly put to one side.

The involvement of Rome in the affairs of Greece was, as Polybius says, also a "beginning" *(katarchē)* which led to a chain of political and military contacts, including in the next generation or so the two Macedonian wars, Flamininus' liberation of Greece, and the defeat of Antiochus III of Syria at Magnesia in 190.[25] These events provoked a flurry of kinship diplomacy, in which the Romans passed from being "barbarians" comparable to the Persians of the fifth century to "descendants of Aeneas" *(Aeneadae)* whose Trojan descent made them the natural protectors of the Greeks rather than their natural enemy. Exactly how this alchemy occurred is now difficult to say, but part of the reason may lie in the ambiguous figure of Aeneas. Not only was he the son and favorite of a goddess whom many ancient peoples recognized and worshipped, but the *Iliad* emphasizes his distance from the house of Priam. After the fall of Troy, he appears in various legends as having betrayed the city to the Greeks or having joined up with Greek heroes such as Odysseus.[26] Aeneas was therefore more suited than any son of Priam, even the noble Hector, to be counted as a Trojan acceptable to Greeks.

In 212 or 211, Rome made alliance with the Greek state of Aetolia against Philip V of Macedon, and the war between the two great powers was to last, with an interval of uneasy peace from 205 to 200, until Philip's defeat at Cynoscephalae in 197. Again, the fragmentary account of Polybius, despite his aversion to considerations of kinship and myth, allows glimpses of their employment in diplomacy. A notable example comes from a time when Rome's intervention in Greece was as yet only a fear. In 217 a conference was held at Naupactus to make peace between Philip and the Aetolians. An Aetolian delegate called Agelaus is credited by Polybius with a speech which probably represents ideas current at the time. Urging Philip to make peace with the Greeks before either Romans or Carthaginians can extend their power eastwards, Agelaus employs an argument which is in some ways reminiscent of Isocrates' letter to Philip II. The young king, so he argues, should care for the Greeks "as if they were his own body . . . and for all parts of Greece as his own intimates and close connections [*hōs oikeioi kai prosēkontes autō*]." Once more the question arises of the precise nuance of *oikeios,* here reinforced by *prosēkōn.* The meaning is surely not that the Greeks are subject to Philip, but especially dear to him. That is, *oikeios* has its diplomatic sense of "familiar," and *prosēkōn,* though it can mean "relative," can likewise refer to a close but not familial relationship, like the Latin *necessarius.*[27]

Soon after Rome's alliance with Aetolia, Aetolian delegates arrived in Sparta to win them for their side, but were countered by the pro-Macedonian Acarnanians. In Polybius' version of their opposing speeches, the Aetolian Chlaeneas reviews Greek relations with Macedon as far back as Philip II in order to make out the Macedonians as enslavers of Greece. A secondary theme is Macedonian impiety, contrasted with the Aetolians' defense of Delphi against the Gauls and of Greece against Macedon.[28] The Acarnanian delegate, Lyciscus, answers his Aetolian counterpart by recalling the philhellenic acts of the Macedonian kings—how Philip II intervened in the Sacred War and rescued Delphi from the Phocians, how Alexander III took vengeance on Persia for its violence against all the Greeks—while the Aetolians plunder holy places and commit deeds worthy of Scythians and Gauls. As for the Romans, he continues:

> With whom are you now sharing your hopes? To what alliance are you inviting those here? One with barbarians, is it not? Do you think your present actions are similar to your

past ones? Aren't they in fact the opposite? For then you contended for primacy against Achaeans and Macedonians of the same kind as yourself [*homophyloi*] and their leader Philip: but now the Greeks are beginning a war for their liberty against strangers [*allophyloi*].

Lyciscus goes on to remind the Spartans of their role in defending Greece against Xerxes, and so underlines the analogy between "the cloud in the west" (an expression which Polybius also attributes to Agelaus in 217) and the Persian invasions. Polybius' readers, and perhaps Lyciscus' auditors, may well have thought of Herodotus' phrase, "so great a cloud of men," applied by Themistocles to the vanquished host of Xerxes.[29] In recounting the debates of 217 and 210, Polybius allows his speakers to invoke kinship and the opposition between barbarism and Hellenism, but not myth, and while that may reflect reality, it is more likely that the historian's discomfort with myth made him select only arguments drawn from the verifiable past.

Polybius does allow mythic arguments to be seen in a transaction of the year 210. The Roman commander in Greece, Publius Sulpicius, had captured the island of Aegina, then in alliance with the Achaeans. "The Aeginetans," says the historian, "begged the proconsul to allow them to send ambassadors to their kinsmen [*syngeneis*] to get ransom. Publius at first gave them a harsh reply, saying that in order to save themselves they should have treated with the stronger party when they were masters of their own fate, not now that they were slaves . . . But the next day he summoned all the captives and said that, though not indebted to the Aeginetans for any favor, still for the sake of the other Greeks he would let them send envoys, since that was the Greek way."[30]

A sharp contrast to Polybius' indifference to myth is provided by a Roman historian contemporary with these events. The patrician senator Fabius Pictor, of the same house (*gens*) as Fabius Maximus, the great adversary of Hannibal, wrote a history of Rome in Greek, which appeared either during the Macedonian war or soon after.[31] In the fashion of Greek historians, Fabius began with an "archaeology" or account of Rome's origins. This certainly included the arrival of Heracles in Italy, and probably also the story of his visit to the site of the future Rome, where he was welcomed by the Arcadian Evander.[32] Fabius also narrated the arrival of Aeneas and his son Ascanius, and perhaps the return of a certain "Lanoius," the eponymous hero of the Latin city of Lanuvium.[33] Similarly, he made a certain Elymus the originator of the Elymoi of western Sicily, in whose territory lay Segesta and Eryx.[34] Fabius is not only Rome's first historian, but may be seen as a literary propagandist in the tradition of Isocrates and fourth-century historians, for example the shadowy Antipater whom Speusippus cited in his *Letter to Philip*.

With the defeat of Hannibal at Zama, and of Philip at Cynoscephalae, Rome had become inextricably involved in the affairs of Greece, and only a few years were to pass before its armies crossed into Asia to confront Antiochus III of Syria. Roman propaganda now entered a new phase. The process whereby descent from Aphrodite and Aeneas made the Romans, if not Greeks, at least philhellenes in the tradition of the defeated Macedonians, was now complete. The great embodiment of this philhellenism, however complex and self-interested his motives may have been, is Titus Flamininus, the victor of Cynoscephalae. After the battle, Flamininus offered two dedications at Delphi. One honored the Dioscuri, the twin sons of Zeus who had helped the Romans at Lake Regillus. "Youths of Zeus, who rejoice in the swift running of horses, sons of Tyndareus [*Tyndaridae*], kings of Sparta, Titus the descendant of Aeneas [*Aeneadas*] has given you a mighty gift after achieving freedom for the sons of the Greeks." The emphasis on descent places Flamininus' services to Greece in the continuum of mythic and historic time, and simultaneously his devotion to the Dioscuri, Greek heroes who had long since arrived in Rome, complements his own Trojan descent. In the corresponding epigram for Apollo, less personal than the first, Flamininus uses the plural, "descendants of Aeneas" *(Aeneadae),* for all the Romans.[35]

The war with Antiochus III of Syria, conducted at first through unfriendly diplomacy and then in open conflict, involved frequent appeals to kinship. After it, myth as a means for small powers to influence great concentrated increasingly on Rome, and in relations between cities was more and more confined to exchanges of ceremony and courtesy. An expressive sign of the new mood is seen in a curious decree of Chios, probably inscribed soon after Antiochus' final defeat. This honors a citizen for displaying "an account of the birth of Romulus the founder of Rome and his brother Remus," probably a series of reliefs, rather as reliefs on the Great Altar of Pergamum show the myth of Telephus, the ancestor of the Pergamenes. As athletic prizes, the Chian benefactor also gave shields inscribed with "myths honoring the Romans," probably not written accounts but rather illustrated scenes from Rome's early history. In all this, he clearly intended to impress the younger citizens with the glorious ancestry and invincible might of Rome.[36]

Rome's newly acquired diplomatic importance is similarly reflected in its relationship with the Lycians, who at some time in the second or first century won the right to call the Romans "friends and kinsmen." Another such "nomination" involves a people of Gaul. In the late 120s the Aedui, situated in modern Burgundy, appealed to Rome for help against two other tribes, the Arverni and the Allobroges, and were honored with what the sources consistently describe as the "name" of brothers or kinsmen (*consanguinei*).[37] No source bases the link on myth or history; on the contrary, a Gallic orator addressing Constantine says explicitly that his people "were believed to be brothers out of simple affection, and deserved to be called so," contrasting their claim with the mythical pretensions of others.[38] This artificial kinship served Caesar as a pretext to go to war outside his province in 58, and the emperor Claudius used the same plea to make a lavish grant of the "broad stripe" *(latus clavus)* to the Aedui, thus permitting their young nobles to enter the Roman senate.[39] In conferring such a title as a courtesy, rather than demanding proofs, the Roman senate gave traditional kinship diplomacy a new form, as a mechanism of empire rather than a currency for the exchange of favors.

This same fusion of Greek forms with Roman is visible in a document, apparently dating to the late republic, and found at Centuripae in east-central Sicily. The Centuripans had despatched ambassadors to Rome, directing them to visit the Latin city of Lanuvium as they returned. On this secondary visit, the envoys obtained a decree acknowledging the "familiarity" (*oikeiosynē,* a word hitherto unattested) between Centuripae and Lanuvium. A mutilated part of the decree has the enigmatic term "colony of the Centuripans," which may refer to some unknown mythic link, but more probably reflects Lanuvium's status as a so-called Latin colony.[40]

The case of Rome has special importance in kinship diplomacy. Like many cities of the ancient world, Rome came to possess a complex of traditions and foundation-legends which could be manipulated in different ways by friends or enemies. The association with Heracles and other heroes such as Odysseus and Evander gave it Hellenic claims, but took second place to the equally old legend of Trojan foundation. The latter was sometimes exploited by enemies such as the Tarentines, but its usefulness was proved in the First Punic War, and thereafter it became paramount, and was reinforced by the ascendance of the Julian house in the first century. For the Greeks, especially those that claimed their own Trojan descent like the Segestans, appeal to such links was certainly motivated by self-interest, but was not, as it has been called, a diplomatic "comedy." Segesta, for one, took the step of deserting the Carthaginians, and was rewarded with years of bitter siege.[41] On the Greek side, myth served to integrate Rome into old patterns of belief, on the Roman to facilitate relations with the empire's new subjects, and it continued to do so even when Rome was no longer a "republic" governed by an oligarchy, but a monarchy under a single prince *(princeps)* or emperor *(imperator).* The transition from republic to principate can be traced in the fortunes of two cities that owed, respectively, resuscitation and birth to the favor of Rome.

8

TWO CITIES

The transition between the republican age of Rome and the imperial, though in one sense it is sharply marked by Octavian's victory at Actium and his metamorphosis four years later into the emperor Augustus, is in another sense a gradual one. Roman historians traced the political events behind the change to the compact of 60 sometimes called the "First Triumvirate." For the Greeks it went back much further, to that day in 200 when the Roman people, responding to appeals from Pergamum and Rhodes, voted war on Philip V of Macedon.[1]

Two cities illustrate both the transition and the practical benefits that were to be gained from alert use of kinship diplomacy. The first is Ilium in the Troad, the successor of the Homeric Troy; the other is Aphrodisias in Caria, not often mentioned in literary texts, but now known in detail because of extraordinary discoveries of archaeology. Unlike the Ilians, the Aphrodisians could not claim kinship with the Romans, but their city was devoted to Aphrodite, the mother of Aeneas, and at some time in the second century it was transformed from a mere agglomeration around the goddess's sanctuary into an independent city, which it remained well into the Byzantine period. It is unlikely that these transformations occurred as a result of the unaided piety of the Romans toward their Trojan ancestors. Though the diplomatic activity which lies behind them is only rarely observable, ambassadors from both cities must constantly have striven to refurbish their city's past links with Rome, as well as asking favors for the future.

After a burst of favor under Alexander and the early successors followed by a decline in the later third century, Ilium began to revive in the first decade of the second. Just as Segesta and Eryx had become trophies in the first Punic War, so was Ilium bound to become one in Rome's struggle with Antiochus III. From Homeric times it contained a celebrated temple of Athena, and in the Hellenistic period this became the religious center of a local league, the League of Athena Ilias.[2] The city had been in the Seleucid sphere in the middle of the previous century, and was bound to Antiochus' family by many ties. As "Antiochus the Great," a monarch claiming descent from Heracles and Apollo, he had no less prestige invested there than did the Romans. We have seen how Roman annalists probably invented the tradition that the Romans had extended their protection to Ilium in the days of a Seleucus, and they are probably responsible for a detail of Livy's account of the peace of Phoenice, which halted hostilities between Rome and Philip in 205. Among the parties included in the terms, Livy lists the Ilians on the Roman side, and he has found many defenders. By his own admission, however, the Romans had had no allies hitherto among Greek cities of Asia, and it was not until very late in the conflict between Rome and Antiochus that the Ilians, tardier than some of their neighbors, resolved to side with Rome.[3]

In the year 197, Antiochus III of Syria began a great campaign to recover his ancestral possessions in Asia Minor. For the Ilian league, the arrival of Antiochus was a critical moment, and one of its members, Lampsacus at the eastern end of the Dardanelles, decided to appeal to Rome. Though Lampsacus was a colony of Phocaea in Ionia, it had close ties with the West. Its sister colonies there included Elea (Velia) in southern Italy, and also Massilia

(Marseilles), which for several decades had been one of Rome's model allies. It was probably, however, as members of the Ilian league that the Lampsacenes considered the Romans their "kinsmen," and accordingly sent a delegation to Rome under a leading citizen, Hegesias. After meeting with Lucius Flamininus, the brother of the liberator, the ambassadors proceeded to their "brothers" in Massilia. Only when the Massilians had agreed to send a supporting delegation did the Lampsacenes come before the senate and beg to be included (though apparently without success) in the treaty currently under negotiation with Philip.[4]

In 190, after the outbreak of war with Antiochus, the consul Lucius Scipio crossed the Hellespont with his army, the first Roman force to touch Asian soil. Like Alexander in 334, Scipio advertised the Romans' claim to be the defenders of Greece against the new Xerxes by duly making the pilgrimage to Ilium, and Livy observes that the citizens "showed every mark of honor in word and deed to proclaim that the Romans were descended from themselves, while the Romans rejoiced in their origin." After Antiochus' defeat, the senate sent ten commissioners to settle the fortunes of the new territories, and these, again in the words of Livy, "gave the Ilians Rhoeteum and Gergithus [two minor towns of the Troad], not so much because of any recent services as in recollection of their origins." So far from having rendered "recent services," the Ilians had supported Antiochus until the last moment, and that the Romans rewarded them with new territory is a measure of their diplomatic skill. At the same time, the commissioners gave freedom to Dardanus to the northeast, lying about halfway between Ilium and Abydus. Their motive was clearly that Aeneas in the *Iliad* and in later tradition had been a ruler of "Dardanians," and the citizens must duly have reminded the commissioners of the fact.[5]

The settlement of 188 marks a turning point in the fortunes of Ilium. A contemporary antiquarian, Demetrius of Scepsis, asserted that when he had visited the city as a youth, "the roofs did not even have tiles," but that it was later transformed by the arrival of the Romans.[6] This sounds in part like the exaggeration of a jealous neighbor, but cannot be entirely false. It was now, it seems, that the League of Athena Ilias began to issue silver coins for use at the festival which the members held every four years in Ilium.[7] Archaeological evidence also suggests a revival of the city in the following decades, when the temple of Athena was rebuilt in pure Hellenistic style.[8] Such a reorganization of the league, together with a rebuilding of its cult center, recalls the senate's measures in Sicily at the end of the First Punic War, and represents the transference to Greek soil of a policy which was to lead to Roman encouragement of provincial councils, and eventually to a council of "all" Greeks, the emperor Hadrian's Panhellenion.

In 133 the last ruler of Pergamum, Attalus III, made the Romans heirs to his kingdom, which in 129 became a Roman province. About the same time, an ancient family of Rome, the Julii, begin to place an image of Venus on their coins, thus advertising a claim which was to have momentous consequences for Ilium. As one of the "Trojan families," the Julii held themselves to be direct descendants of Aeneas and Aphrodite.[9] In 89 Lucius Julius Caesar, only distantly related to the dictator, became responsible as censor for letting out the contract for taxes to the tax-farmers *(publicani)*. An inscription found at Ilium shows that he "restored the sacred land to Athena Ilias," or in other words exempted it from Roman taxation.[10] His son of the same name also intervened as quaestor in the affairs of the league, apparently bringing them into financial order.[11]

Though the Julii were to be decisive for Ilium's future, another patron may have seemed more valuable at the time. Much of our knowledge of Sulla's personality comes from the biographer Plutarch, who acknowledges the Roman's devotion to the goddess Aphrodite, but is much more interested in his plundering of Delphi and the Academy. The documentary record, by contrast, suggests a great philhellene in the line of Flamininus, eager to promote sanctuaries like the Amphiaraon of Oropus in Greece. As consul for 88, Sulla was appointed to prosecute the war with Mithridates VI of Pontus, then at the height of his power in Asia and Greece. It is unknown whether Mithridates, imitating Xerxes and Antiochus III, had made exceptional efforts to win over Ilium, but the city appears to have gone over to his side.[12] When the Roman legate, Flavius Fimbria, appeared before the city, he demanded admittance, "making ironic remarks about the kinship between Romans and Ilians"; while the Ilians were appealing to Sulla, Fimbria proceeded to sack the city, which in Appian's words "perished at the hands of a kinsman, receiving worse treatment from him than from Agamemnon." Eager to repair the damage to Roman prestige, Sulla contributed generously to the city's restoration,[13] and to the same context of postwar recovery belong the measures of the younger Lucius Caesar on behalf of the Ilian league.

With the dictator Gaius Caesar, of the younger branch of the family, Ilium entered into a period of prosperity that was to continue unbroken into the principate. Writing under Augustus and Tiberius, Strabo has no doubt that kinship explained these favors:

In my day [Julius] Caesar favored [the Ilians] much more [than Sulla had done], at the same time competing with Alexander; for the latter began to favor them because of a renewal of kinship, and at the same time as an admirer of Homer . . . but Caesar, being both an admirer of Alexander and having the most incontrovertible proofs of kinship with the Ilians, was very energetic in his benefactions; incontrovertible, first because he was a Roman, and the Romans consider Aeneas their founder [*archēgetēs*], and second because he was a Julius descended from an ancestor called Iulus . . . and by ancestry was one of those descended from Aeneas. He gave them therefore land, and helped them protect their freedom and immunity, possessions which they still preserve.[14]

Curiously, while detailing the lavish benefactions of Julius Caesar toward the city, Strabo fails to mention those of Augustus, which are much more apparent in the archaeological record. As is now known from excavation, Augustus restored the temple of

Athena Ilias and probably contributed toward the city's new concert hall *(ōdeion)* and council chamber *(bouleutērion)*.[15] A series of statue-bases shows the city honoring Augustus and members of his family down to Nero as "cousins" *(syngeneis)*. By a curious etiquette, individual citizens could not use this language of members of the imperial house, though they could call them "benefactor" or even "guest."[16]

Such cousins could be dangerous. When Julia, the daughter of Augustus and wife of Agrippa, was caught in a sudden flood on her way to the city, Agrippa punished the city with a huge fine. Only by imploring Nicolaus of Damascus, the agent of Herod of Judaea, could the citizens win forgiveness from the emperor's son-in-law.[17]

Nero's relations with Ilium are known from the pages of Tacitus. While still Claudius' stepson, he launched his public career by a speech before the senate in which he obtained the exemption of the city from all public taxes. Tacitus ironically notes that the imperial orator based his plea on the descent of the Romans from Troy and on other "ancient matters little less than fables," but Nero was only articulating motives which had governed Rome's relations with Ilium from the beginning. We shall see Caracalla on his entry into public life bestowing similar favors on Aphrodisias, and such acts were no doubt considered a harmless way for princes to gain general approval.[18]

On the present evidence, these close contacts between the ruling house and the city of Ilium end with the Julio-Claudian dynasty, perhaps because its successors no longer claimed descent from the patrician house of the Julii, even though they retained the name of Caesar. While the city may not have declined, it was overshadowed by the prosperous Roman colony of Alexandria Troas to the south.[19] In this, its fortunes contrast with those of a city which in other ways received similar treatment from the Romans, Aphrodisias in Caria.[20]

For Aphrodisias, the crucial moment appears to have arrived in the year 167, when the Romans deprived their Rhodian allies of their sovereignty over Lycia and Caria. Using the occasion to adjust the status of the cities affected, they increased the territory of Antioch on the Maeander, Aphrodisias' neighbor to the north.[21] Either on this occasion or later in the century, they elevated what had hitherto been a rural sanctuary of Aphrodite to the status of a city in political union *(sympoliteia)* with the neighboring town of Plarasa. A marble altar surviving from this period shows that the new creation joined with Tabae, some thirty kilometers to the south, and Cibyra, about a hundred kilometers to the southeast, in a treaty of "alliance, everlasting concord, and brotherhood." Since the oath was taken in the name of the goddess Roma and involved an undertaking not to act against Roman interests, it appears that Rome wished to establish a federation in eastern Caria with Aphrodisias as its focus, much as it had used Eryx as a focus for Sicilian loyalty.[22]

For the rest of the republican period, the fortunes of Aphrodisias in several ways resemble those of Ilium. A major exception is the first war between Rome and Mithridates of Pontus, for though Ilium appears to have gone over to the king, Aphrodisias, owing its existence to the Romans, was unswerving in their support. Soon after Sulla arrived in Greece to prosecute the war, he received an oracle from Delphi which promised victory to the race of Aeneas and ordered him to dedicate an ax at Aphrodisias "beneath snowy Taurus." With his customary piety, Sulla did more than he was ordered, and sent not only an ax but a gold crown as well. The symbolism of this double gift refers to the combined polity of Plarasa and Aphrodisias. The ax is the symbol of Carian Zeus, and a frequent device on the coins of Plarasa, while gold, though appropriate for all the immortals, is traditionally associated with Aphrodite by the epithet "golden," frequent in Homer and in later poets. For the same reason, Sicilians loyal to Rome wore gold in honor of Venus of Eryx.[23]

Like Ilium, Aphrodisias received benefits from Julius Caesar. One, appropriately, was a golden Eros which he dedicated to the goddess, and he appears to have given, or to have extended, the sacred immunity *(asylia)* of the sanctuary.[24] A recently reconstituted monument of the city honors a benefactor who guided its fortunes in the troubled years of the late republic. He is Gaius Julius Zoilus, a freedman of either Caesar or Augustus. Among the figures of myth and allegory carved in relief are the goddess Roma, symbolizing Zoilus' links with Rome, and also Minos of Crete. This second image does not only celebrate Zoilus' reception into the underworld, where Minos, once the king of a great sea empire, was now a judge. It probably also recalls the link of kinship claimed by many Carian cities with Crete.[25] Zoilus may well have been one of those Aphrodisian ambassadors who reminded eminent Romans of the links of myth between his city and theirs.

Even more than Ilium, Aphrodisias continued to prosper in the imperial period. A monument from the middle of the first century shows the power of Greek myth to integrate the city into a world ruled by Rome. An avenue was built by leading families of the city to lead up to the temple of the ruling house, or Sebasteion. On either side stood three-storied porticos, with relief panels in the upper two. The north portico displayed Rome as a world conqueror, enumerating the tribes conquered by Augustus. The middle story on the south side displayed a variety of myths, none of which seem closely related to the city; but the upper story advertised the relationship of Aphrodisias to the imperial house. Here panels depicted the birth of Eros (half brother to Aeneas), Aeneas' flight from Troy, his descendants Romulus and Remus being suckled by the wolf, and probably the city-goddess of Aphrodisias crowned by Rome. The overall intention was surely to suggest the blessings brought on the world by Aphrodite, and channeled toward her own city by the piety of her descendants.[26]

Despite the warm relationship between Aphrodisias and Rome, there is a noticeable difference from Ilium in the language with which that relationship is described, and this contrast shows clearly the difference between the diplomatic terms *syngenēs,* "kindred," and *oikeios,* "familiar" or "intimate." The citizens of Ilium refer to the early emperors as kinsmen because of their common link through the house of Priam, but the Aphrodisians make no claim of kinship either with Aphrodite or with the

Romans. When they honor her as *promētōr*, "female ancestor," they do so exclusively as ancestor of the imperial house.

One example of this protocol comes from the Sebasteion already mentioned. The forecourt of this complex contained a number of statue-bases, one of which honored Aphrodite as the "ancestor of the Augusti," while another honored "Aeneas son of Anchises."[27] Other statues are for various members of the family of Augustus, Tiberius and Gaius.[28] The inclusion of Aphrodite and Aeneas in the complex shows that this was the relationship that mattered. The lack of direct kinship between Rome and Aphrodisias made no difference to the favor which the city enjoyed from the Julio-Claudian and later emperors. As long as the emperors remained pagan, it continued to profit from the Roman reverence for Aphrodite.

A similar case involves the emperor Trajan. An Aphrodisian statue-base once held a group showing the giants called Cyclopes, and the text declares that the emperor restored the statues in honor of his "ancestor" Aphrodite. The funds for the restoration were bequeathed by a prominent citizen, and his heirs or the city must have obtained the emperor's permission to restore the statue-group in his name, reminding him of their worship of his ancestral goddess.[29]

As well as the Sebasteion, a glory of the excavated site is the theater. Beginning in the Severan era, the Aphrodisians inscribed several walls of the north entrance-way *(parodos)* with documents showing the favor of Roman generals and emperors toward them. These texts do not constitute an archive, as was at first thought, but a selection of documents, doubtless drawn from the civic archives and set up for the benefit of citizens and visitors.[30] We would expect these letters to make frequent mention of the kinship between Rome and the goddess Aphrodite, but they do not begin to do so until the reign of Septimius Severus, the founder of the dynasty. The explanation is clearly that such references were called for in diplomatic documents of a particular kind— confirmatory letters which emperors wrote at the beginning of their rule to thank the city for its congratulations, and to confirm its existing privileges. When inscribing the correspondence of earlier emperors on the wall, the Aphrodisians omitted such letters as irrelevant to their purpose.[31]

The first of such confirmatory letters belongs to the year 198. The city had, it appears, congratulated Severus and Caracalla on their recent successes over the Parthians.[32] Their reply is lacunose, but it begins: "It was entirely likely that, since you reverence the goddess from whom the nobility . . ." The word "nobility" *(eugeneia)* recurs often in connection with a city's descent from gods and heroes, though it is no less frequent in praise of persons.[33] As descendants of Aphrodite and Aeneas, the Romans could claim their own "nobility" *(nobilitas)*. Thus the emperor Justinian says of Caracalla, who extended the Roman citizenship to all free inhabitants of the empire, that he brought them "into Roman nobility" *(Rhōmaikē eugeneia)*.[34] In the letter of Severus and Caracalla, the nobility to which the emperors refer is their own or the Romans', not that of Aphrodisias. Their language shows how far an old Greek concept had been assimilated to a Roman one, and how diplomacy between a Greek city and Rome was facilitated by these shared values.

In another letter from the same two emperors which appears to be slightly later, Caracalla is the principal author. The language is very similar: "It was fitting that you should rejoice at my succeeding to partnership with my father . . . since you are more closely connected [*prosēkontes*] to the Roman empire than others through the goddess who presides over your city."[35] We have already met the word here translated "connected," *prosēkōn*, in the speech of Agelaus to Philip V, where it was combined with *oikeios* and appeared to mean not "relative," but "closely linked."[36] In the present case, a reference to blood relationship is excluded by the following "to the Roman empire."

A letter of Gordian III, written soon after his accession, similarly fails to refer to kinship between Aphrodisias and Rome. The emperor ascribes three qualities to the Aphrodisians, their antiquity *(archaiotēs)*, goodwill *(eunoia)*, and friendship *(philia)* toward the Romans, but he makes no mention of kinship with the goddess, either his own or that of the citizens.[37] A letter of Decius and his son Herennius Etruscus, written soon after Herennius' elevation to the rank of Augustus in mid-250, is more eloquent. "Both because of the goddess who has given her name to your city, and because of your familiarity [*oikeiotēs*] and fidelity [*pistis*] toward the Romans, it was right that you should rejoice at the establishment of our rule and offer the appropriate sacrifices and prayers."[38] This last phrase is probably a discreet allusion to the worship of the traditional gods which Decius had recently ordered in this same year, thus launching the so-called Decian persecution of the Christians. It is all the more notable that the two emperors say nothing either of their own or of the Aphrodisians' kinship with the goddess, but speak only of the city's "familiarity" with the Romans. As early as the fifth century, this term refers rather to the closeness of a relationship between states than to any specific kinship. In the imperial period, it appears among the official titles of certain cities, in the form "familiar with the emperors" *(oikeia tōn autokratorōn)*. Like Aphrodisias, these cities have no link of blood with the emperor, but plume themselves on their "special relationship" with him.[39]

From the comparison of these two cities, two principal conclusions emerge for kinship diplomacy. One concerns the scrupulous care which cities and rulers took to observe correct forms. The Ilians may collectively, but not individually, refer to the emperors as "kinsmen." The Aphrodisians do not claim for themselves that descent from gods and heroes which belongs to the Romans, in the imperial period to the emperors. The other conclusion, related to the first, involves the material advantages to be drawn from such relationships. For Ilium, the best evidence comes from literary texts, from Strabo and Tacitus, who attest to the benefits conferred on the city by Julius Caesar and Nero respectively as descendants of Aeneas. For Aphrodisias, the evidence is wholly archaeological. Tacitus, in his sole reference to the city, mentions only its support of Julius Caesar and its loyalty to Augustus as a source of Roman favor.[40] No doubt considerations of loyalty and past conduct were always important, and as late as 250 Decius and his son recall the city's fidelity toward the Romans. How much they weighed in the scale by contrast with considerations of kinship and "familiarity" no doubt varied from case to case.

Throughout its history, Ilium was subject to raids from the sea. Even in the Julio-Claudian period, when it was basking in imperial favor, it was prey to pirate attacks.[41] This danger can only have grown in the later third century, as Goths and others sailed with ease and frequency through the Hellespont. By contrast, Aphrodisias gives every sign of having continued to flourish well into late antiquity. Its associations with the goddess Aphrodite were by that time no longer of value. What the city had instead was, first, a secure site, well away from the sea and the Maeander valley, and well protected by stout walls; second, flourishing industries, particularly those based on the nearby marble quarries. Perhaps these advantages would ultimately have raised it to prominence, even without the lucky coincidence that the fertility goddess worshipped there from early times became identified with the mother of the Romans. But it was surely that coincidence that brought the city to birth in the first place, and then sustained it for some four centuries, until it could survive as a mother city (mētropolis) in its own right.

9

THE ROMAN EMPIRE

Though Augustus' establishment of monarchy at Rome was in one sense merely the political expression of slower and deeper changes in the Roman empire, still its effects were immediate, and obvious to contemporaries. Greek observers of the new era noted that cities could no longer conduct their own foreign policy. "Formerly," says Strabo early in the principate, "they used to deliberate about war, peace, and alliance, but that is not likely now; these things inevitably depend on the Romans."[1] Embassies might still go to the governor of a province, but their chief target was the emperor, often called the "king," whether he was in the capital or abroad. If he referred them to the senate, he did so in deference to times past, to an "image of antiquity."[2]

From the establishment of Roman power in Macedonia and Greece in the second century, Rome had tended to favor the few over the many, restricting the power of the popular assemblies and reinforcing such institutions as the city councils *(boulai)* or, even more, exclusive bodies like the Areopagus of Athens. Influential citizens enjoying Rome's favor, men like Diodorus Pasparus of Pergamum, thus became in large part the successors of the kings who had once ruled over their cities, or peers of the kings who survived as Roman dependents. Though no longer applicable to the wars or rivalries of great powers, diplomacy remained a powerful tool in the hands of local elites. The same people who pleaded the heroic ancestry of their cities might claim their own descent from local heroes.[3] Alternatively, outstanding citizens might be compared to heroes by the people, who were now reduced to expressing their wishes and hopes through shouts or "acclamations." A wealthy man who had supplied his compatriots with grain might be hailed as a "new Triptolemus," a reincarnation of the hero who first taught humanity how to cultivate cereals.[4]

While diplomatic intercourse continued between cities, sometimes between a city and a king dependent for his power on Rome, appeals to kinship were much rarer than before. The circumstances that had provoked them in the Hellenistic era, calls for help against enemies or for recognition of immunity, had largely vanished. If such dangers still existed, recourse was now to be had to the imperial house, as when the city of Ilium appealed to an imperial agent for help against pirates.[5] But diplomacy between cities no longer seemed so worth recording on stone as other deeds of powerful citizens, such as a successful embassy to Rome or the gift of grain in a time of shortage.

Even if rarely noted in diplomacy between cities, however, kinship in an age of moral and religious revival remained a powerful tool for cities in their dealings with Rome. In addition, the victory of Augustus meant that such pleas had no longer to be diffused among a variety of governors, generals, and patrons, but could be focused on one person and his immediate entourage. This individualization of power also brought its drawbacks. Even a city basking in imperial favor might incur the royal "anger," which could be averted only by further diplomatic efforts, as when the Ilians inadvertently offended the princess Julia.[6]

From the Flavian period on, a signal feature of public life in both East and West is the fierce rivalry between cities, intensified by competition for privileges and titles. This is less obvious under the Julio-Claudians, perhaps because the cities were still too busy recovering from the effects of civil war. Nonetheless, the dark chronicler of the first dynasty, the historian Tacitus, noted in a later age the symptoms of an illness that was soon to beset the Greek world. His account of the reign of Tiberius includes some revealing transactions about the provinces of Achaea and Asia, in which he seems to have had a particular interest.[7]

In the Hellenistic period, the issue of "inviolability" *(asylia)* had in large part involved the protection of holy places, sometimes whole cities, from acts of war and piracy. In the late republic, it assumed more and more the character of a civic honor and a financial advantage, as cities obtained from Roman warlords or from the senate recognition of their most notable sanctuaries as immune from the jurisdiction of governors and the demands of tax-collectors. After the victory of Augustus, these privileges came into conflict with a basic tenet of the new empire, its insistence on the "tranquillity" of the subject provinces, and the avoidance at all costs of disturbance and disorder. An example is provided by Ephesus and its sanctuary of Artemis, which stood outside the city to the northeast. Warmly disposed toward the Ephesians, Antony extended the radius of the goddess's inviolability so that it included part of the urban area. In the eyes of Augustus, this put the city at the mercy of criminals, who were able to evade Roman jurisdiction by resorting to the protection of the goddess, and the emperor therefore reduced the area of inviolability to the actual sanctuary.[8]

In the year 22, no doubt moved by concerns similar to his divine father's, Tiberius ordered a general review of all such claims. Tacitus mentions about fifteen cases from provinces that were regarded as being specially within the purview of the senate, above all the province of Asia. Those cities that wished to maintain their inviolability had to present their claims to the conscript fathers, and the arguments used ranged from the earliest myths down to the reign of Augustus.

The leading case was that of Ephesus, which appears to have claimed inviolability for two different sites, the sanctuary of Artemis, just outside the city, and the sacred grove of Ortygia, about five hours by ancient travel to the south.[9] This last the Ephesians defended as the place where Leto had given birth to Apollo and Artemis, and where Apollo had fled to avoid the anger of his father, Zeus. Similarly, the altar before the temple of Artemis had sheltered the Amazons from the anger of Dionysus. As in Speusippus' *Letter to Philip,* the Ephesians cited myth not just for its antiquity, but because it showed gods and heroes acting in ways that provided models for humankind. If Zeus and Dionysus had respected the inviolability of these shrines, that was a moral consideration which might sway the Roman senate. At the same time, the background of the Ephesians' plea was crucially different from the menacing instability that lay behind the letter of Speusippus.[10]

The same issue of local pride emerges even more clearly in a slightly later transaction, the competition among cities of Asia to house their newly decreed temple of Tiberius, Livia, and the senate.[11] As in the question of inviolability, the arguments which the cities presented to the emperor and senate involved both remote antiquity and recent history, though with this difference, that the issue turned not on considerations of security but on imperial prestige. Cities that seemed too slight for the majesty of the proposed temple were passed over. Among these was Ilium, which made the same argument it had used with the Romans on their first arrival in Asia, the descent of Rome from Troy and the kinship between the two cities. This time, myth took second place to more practical considerations.

At the final stage of the competition, the rivals were Sardis and Smyrna. The envoys of Sardis read out a decree of their "kinsmen" *(consanguinei)* the Etruscans, which recounted a legend very close to one in Herodotus, that Etruria had been colonized by the Lydian prince Tyrrhenus. Though forged documents were sometimes used in pleas of kinship, there is no reason to suspect this one. The ancient Etruscan league was reconstituted under the early empire, probably by Augustus, and the Sardians must have approached it before coming before the senate, exactly as Lampsacus had approached its sister colony of Massilia before addressing the senate in 196.[12] Nor is it a surprise that Etruria was worth claiming as kindred territory. Its history was intimately connected with that of Rome, and many members of the ruling class had Etruscan connections by birth or marriage. At the time of the Sardian plea, one of these influential Etruscans was none other than Tiberius' all-powerful minister, Sejanus. The envoys had another argument to show their ancient wealth and kinships, for Pelops, the mythical king of Lydia, had sent settlers to Greece, and given his name to the Peloponnese, the "Island of Pelops."

The competition was won by Smyrna, the third city of Asia after Ephesus and Pergamum, which could show a consistent record of loyalty to Rome, dating back to the war with Antiochus III. Its case may also have been aided by the eloquence of its envoys, for in the next generation its schools of rhetoric were destined to lead the way to that great revival of oratory which history knows as the Second Sophistic.[13] Ultimately, however, what may have decided the issue were Smyrna's favorable situation on the coast of Asia and its greater ability to maintain the expenses of the imperial cult. Once again, pleas of kinship yielded before ones of practical advantage.

From the earliest times, the Greeks had used myth to establish or justify territorial claims, as when Speusippus justified Philip's conquests by his descent from Heracles. Similar arguments could still be made in the changed atmosphere of the Tiberian senate. In the southwestern Peloponnese, lying between Laconia and Messenia, was a fertile region called the "Dentheliate land," on which stood a venerable temple of Artemis in the Marshes. This region was an ancient bone of contention between Sparta and Messene. Geographically it was closer to Messenia than to Laconia, but it had several times changed hands by force or adjudication.[14] One of these occasions, which can be dated about 140, is known from an inscription found at Olympia. A contending party, probably Sparta, brought the matter to the Roman senate, which referred it to Miletus. After hearing both sides, the Milesian assembly voted by a large majority in favor of Messene, which prevailed on its "kinsmen," the Eleans, to have the matter recorded in their great sanctuary. At the time of the hearing under Tiberius, a Roman governor had recently restored the land to Messene, but Sparta appealed his decision to the emperor. He in turn referred it to the senate, just as he had done with the question of civic inviolability.[15]

The situation of 26 presents a striking contrast with that of the second century, since the two legations argued the case not before the public assembly of a Greek city, but before the senate of Rome. At the same time, the arguments once more show the continuity that was felt to exist between mythic and historic times. Though the Spartans appealed to historians and poets to prove their foundation of the temple, they could produce only a single decision in their favor. The Messenians, for their part, resorted to the familiar argument of the conquests of Heracles and their distribution among his descendants. To prove that their own first king had received the land as a gift from the hero, they cited "records carved on rocks and on ancient bronze" and also texts of literature.[16] They could also produce a series of favorable rulings, from the time of Philip II of Macedon down to the recent governor. Like the question of inviolability, the issue turned partly on the appeal to antiquity and to the precedent created by gods and heroes, in this case Heracles. As before, Tacitus gives every sign of regarding the dispute as a real one, perhaps because it had arisen again in his own lifetime.[17]

From his account of the temple of Artemis in the Marshes, Tacitus proceeds to the subject of a temple much better known in Roman history, the one of Venus at Eryx. At some unknown date, Segesta had gained control of this shrine, which had now fallen into disrepair. The city therefore appealed to the emperor for help in restoring it, "mentioning well-known facts, likely to please Tiberius, about its origins, and he gladly undertook the burden as a kinsman [*consanguineus*]."[18] The "well-known facts" were doubtless above all a tradition immortalized by Vergil, according to which the temple was founded by none other than

Aeneas. Even Tacitus, for all his irony, is still interested in the effect that kinship diplomacy could have on a Roman emperor
who claimed descent from the Trojan hero.

Though the cities of old Greece had recovered from the rav-
ages of the civil war by the time of the Flavian dynasty, in wealth
and vitality they fell more and more behind those of Asia Minor,
especially those of the Aegean seaboard.[19] There now began the
period that Edward Gibbon referred to as the "meridian splen-
dour" of the Roman empire. In literature, this is particularly associated with the public speakers whom the Younger Philostratus
grouped together in his "Second Sophistic." While Philostratus
did not intend this term as a tool of historical analysis, it serves to
illuminate a period extending from the later first century to the
middle of the third, when men of culture such as the Athenian
Herodes Atticus flourished and, in many cases, reaped the advantages of Roman rule.[20]

Not the least manifestation of this period is an intense interest
in spirituality and religion, whether a revival of older forms or
the invention of new ones. Examples of the latter are two targets
of the satirist Lucian, Peregrinus of Parium and Alexander of
Abonuteichos. The high valuation placed on verbal dexterity, and
the interest in religion, especially as expressed in old forms, now
coalesce to intensify the traffic in myth. As in the early empire,
diplomacy continues to flow principally toward the emperors,
wherever they may be. The city of Rome, by contrast, recedes in
importance both as a diplomatic goal and in the complex of myth.

Diplomacy between cities has also undergone changes. The
main issue is now no longer the cities' need for mutual assistance.
The overriding concern is with prestige *(axiōma, doxa)*, precedence *(prōteia, prostasia, propompeia)*, and rights *(dikaia)*. These
quarrels often lead to strife *(stasis)*, whose opposite is concord
(homonoia), a state which often can be achieved only by the stren-
uous intervention of emperors and governors. Another major
change is that diplomacy is now conducted not between demo-
cratically constituted cities but by a political elite. One well-
chosen ambassador can accomplish as much as the large delega-

tions of earlier times, especially if he has a long and expensive education in literature and rhetoric, or counts highly placed Romans among his friends. Thus Plutarch, in his *Political Precepts,* envisages civic embassies, for example to another city on the subject of concord, consisting of only one or two persons.[21]

This is sometimes seen as a period of archaism or of refuge from the present, but is better regarded as an exaltation of classical models in literature and art, an obliviousness not so much of the present as of the intervening past, especially the Hellenistic period with its sorry tale of Macedonian overlordship and of Greek decadence. Nor was such a revival confined to Greek or Latin. This era saw the reappearance of documents in such languages as Punic, and of religious traditions which had been dormant for centuries. If the record of diplomatic activity is now much sparser than in Hellenistic times, the change reflects a loss of communal consciousness to the profit of upper-class solidarity. Only when a person of wealth and culture undertakes to concern himself with diplomacy, often also paying for the cost of commemorating his achievements on stone, does his activity leave a permanent record.

Three cases may be considered. Stratonicea was now one of the leading cities of Caria.[22] Already in the late Hellenistic period, its temple of Hecate at nearby Lagina was one of the chief shrines of the region. Another of its sanctuaries, Panamara, was dedicated to the god of the Carians customarily identified with Zeus. The many inscriptions show that the annual rite in which the god's image was carried to and from the city attracted visitors from far and wide, including Roman senators.[23] Though cities of Caria were presumably always invited, at some time in the second century a priest of Zeus decided to record in stone the invitations which he had sent to kindred cities.[24] The letter addressed to Rhodes is the best preserved:

Even if the god invites all mankind to the banquet, and provides a general feast of equal honor to those who arrive from anywhere, nevertheless I consider your city worthy of spe-

cial honor, Rhodians, because of your repute [*axiōma*], because of the kinship [*syngeneia*] that exists between our cities,
and because of our shared rites. I invite you, then, to the
god, and I invite those in your city to join the revelry at his
shrine, as I do those Rhodians who are our neighbors in
Caria. It will be a great honor [*timē*] for us if you receive this
letter with pleasure, and indicate as much to the god.[25]

All the other letters which are more than fragments refer in
similar terms to kinship with Stratonicea,[26] and all are within
Caria except Rhodes and Miletus. Rhodes, as the priest's letter
makes clear, was in effect a Carian city because of its large territory on the mainland, though he may also have been thinking of
the tradition that the Carians had once inhabited the islands of the
Aegean. Miletus, though usually reckoned as Ionian, is a Carian
city in the Homeric Catalogue of Ships.[27]

A similar story is told by a curious document, probably also of
the second century, from a small city of southwestern Lycia called
Sidyma. This too is a letter, sent by the magistrates of Tlos in the
Xanthus valley, and couched in an even more recondite language
than the letter of the Carian priest. It records the discourse of a
certain Hieron, a citizen of Tlos and of other cities, who has lec-
tured the town council of Sidyma on the links uniting the city
with Tlos, illustrating his points with earlier "renewals of kinship"
and with extracts from historians. To trace these ties from their
beginning, Hieron resorts to the familiar schema of eponymous
founders related as father and son, in this case Tlous and Sidymus,
a device which respectfully acknowledges the priority of the senior city. "Thus from gods and indigenous founders," he argues,
"we have a unity and concord with the Sidymans like that between children and parents, unbroken under every circum-
stance."[28] The orator proceeds to describe another link between
the cities. At an unknown date, an oracle of Apollo had ordered
the Sidymans to select children born of marriages between citizens of both cities, with the intention that they should serve the
god's sister, Artemis, at Tlos.

Like the priest of Zeus at Stratonicea, Hieron of Tlos employs his mannered Greek to recall myths extending back to a time before the coming of the Greeks. In his scheme, Tlous, the eponym of Tlos and the father of Sidymus, is the son of a certain Tremiles, the eponym of the "Termilai," the original name of the Lycians in their own language.[29] As at Stratonicea, a single well-placed citizen ensures the good relations between two communities with which he has connections, and once again, it may well be the same benefactor who paid for the inscribing of his own speech.

A third case recalls the appeal which Xerxes makes to Argos in Herodotus, claiming descent from the Argive hero Perseus. This time, however, the claim is made by a sophist called Antiochus from the city of Aegeae in Cilicia. This allegedly owed its foundation to Alexander of Macedon, but enters into history only in the late republican period. Down to the late empire it was a flourishing port, famous for its healing sanctuary of the god Asclepius.[30] Like many other cities of Asia Minor, especially those along the less Hellenized coasts on the north and south, Aegeae used the myth of Perseus' wanderings to affirm its links to old Greece.[31]

Such ties, however, were liable to lapse unless carefully maintained by diplomacy, and admittance to the society of cities founded by gods or heroes of ancient Greece often required elaborate proof. But whereas the city of Apollonia in Mysia had sent an official delegation to renew its ties with Miletus, it is characteristic of the high empire that a single citizen of Aegeae, a sophist, undertook the task. His success is recorded in an inscription of Argos, which through Perseus counted as the mother city of Aegeae.[32] Lecturing in Argos, Antiochus took the opportunity to "recall the ties" between the two cities by a display of his "perfection in culture." For this purpose he regaled the local authorities with an exposition of mythic history in a manner very similar to Hieron of Tlos. In Antiochus' telling, Perseus as he wandered in search of the Gorgon had come to Cilicia, "the extreme limit of Asia."[33] He was carrying an image, perhaps of Athena, copied from an original in Argos, and deposited this copy in Aegeae, thus planting the cult on new soil.

It is a reasonable guess, though the text does not say so, that Antiochus belonged to the local aristocracy of Aegeae, whose members traced their ultimate origin to Argos. It was no novelty for the diplomacy of kinship to be conducted by persons who traced their origin back to distant heroes of their city—the Callias of fourth-century Athens who cited the precedent of his ancestor Triptolemus is an early example. But this tendency is more marked in a period when civic affairs were largely in the hands of a small élite, the "politicians" *(politeuomenoi),* since these usually came from a city's long-established families.

It is therefore curious that kinship is not more frequently connected with a widespread phenomenon of Greek civic life under the empire, the search for "concord." This ideal receives much praise from contemporary speakers like Dio Chrysostom and Aelius Aristides, and is frequent in coins and inscriptions of the second and third centuries.[34] Yet of the many coins that represent "concord" between two or sometimes three cities, none mentions kinship, and there is perhaps only one case in which the concept is represented pictorially. This is a series of issues, going from Pius down to Valerian, which mark the good relations between Mytilene and Pergamum. (See Figure 3.) Clearly struck in Mytilene, they show the city goddess being greeted by a figure representing Pergamum—the personified city, the eponymous hero Pergamus, or the god Asclepius. The bond between Pergamum and Mytilene was very ancient, and remained vital in the imperial period. A typical document of it is a Mytilenean inscription, written in an archaizing Aeolic, which honors a wealthy Pergamene who performed civic duties both in his own city and in the "kindred" Mytilene.[35] Similarly, the only inscription mentioning concord in the context of kinship seems to be one in which a Roman colony of central Asia Minor, Lystra in Lycaonia, honors its "sister," Antioch by Pisidia, with a statue marking their "concord."[36]

The reverse of "concord" is "faction" *(stasis),* and probably many of the coins and inscriptions just discussed are intended to mark the absence or the settlement of quarrels between cities.

Figure 3. Coin of Mitylene from reign of Valerian,

One of the duties of the "politician" was to prevent such disputes, and on at least one occasion kinship diplomacy played a part. A sophist called Marcus of Byzantium claimed descent from Byzas, the eponymous founder of his city, and was thus welcome in Megara, of which Byzantium was a colony. On one such visit, he found that the Megarians, still pursuing their ancient quarrel with their Athenian neighbors, had excluded them from their Pythian games. Nonetheless, according to Philostratus, "he so swayed the Megarians that he persuaded them to open up their houses, and to introduce the Athenians to their wives and children."[37]

At first sight, it seems incredible that Megara should still be nursing a grievance that went back six centuries. But this incident is fully consistent with an aspect of diplomacy which is especially conspicuous in the second century, quarrels over rights and titles which often could be settled only by the emperor or the senate. It is not by chance that such disputes often involved the right to be called "mother city," since much prestige flowed from being acknowledged either as a local capital or as the founder of far-distant colonies.[38] If Sardis was now "first metropolis of Asia,

Lydia and Hellas," that seems to be because its first king was a son of Zeus and Earth *(Gē),* and because Pelops had colonized the Peloponnese, a claim which the Sardians had previously rehearsed before the Tiberian senate.[39] Often such titles are qualified with a phrase like "according to the decrees of the senate" or "according to the judgment of emperors." Cities were probably always required to submit such claims to Rome, but this ostentatious mention covers something more—a diplomatic triumph over some rival.[40]

Nor is this a phenomenon confined to cities closely connected with old Greece. In the eastern Mediterranean, Laodicea by the Sea called itself, among other titles, "ruler of the sea [*nauarchis*], kindred [*syngenis*], friend, ally, and partner of the Roman people." The epithets reflect Laodicea's loyalty to Julius Caesar in the civil wars and, probably, the presence of Roman settlers among the population.[41] It exemplifies a cultural difference between such eastern cities and those of Greece and western Asia Minor that they were not reluctant to evoke Hellenistic kings as founders, or even Roman generals such as Pompey.[42]

An institution which typifies this thirst of second-century cities for recognition of their ancient kinship is the Panhellenion, founded about 131, doubtless at Hadrian's prompting.[43] This was in large part a religious league, based in Athens or Eleusis, whose two chief functions were the cult of Hadrian and his successors, and the maintenance of a contest held every fourth year, the Panhellenia. Though its name proclaimed it as a union of "all Greeks," it was far from being a parliament of all Greeks everywhere. There is no sign that the chief cities of the province of Asia—Ephesus, Smyrna, and Pergamum—were members, nor any of the ancient Greek communities in Sicily or Italy. Instead, cities appear to have gained entrance to the Panhellenion only if they were prepared to accept the cultural primacy of Athens, Sparta, and other capitals of Hellenism on the Greek mainland.

For those who did make this concession, however, the creation of the Panhellenion brought intense diplomacy, directed at proving their membership in the commonwealth of Greeks. Thus

Magnesia on the Maeander, which had conducted such a vigorous campaign for the recognition of its local games in the Hellenistic period, duly applied for membership. It then proudly inscribed at Athens the answer which it received from the board of Panhellenes. At the head of the text stands not the word "Gods" as is usual in such documents, but the name "Leucippus," the hero who led the Magnesians to their final place of settlement in Asia.[44] The opening lines of the decree run:

> Whereas the Magnesians of the Maeander, being colonists [*apoikoí*] of the Magnesians in Thessaly, the first of Greeks to cross into Asia and settle there, who also fought valiantly on many occasions beside the Ionians, Dorians, and the Aeolians (who were of their own race [*genos*]) in Asia, also honored by the Roman people for the alliance which they made with it, who have received conspicuous gifts from the emperor Hadrian, the father of Titus Aelius Caesar . . .

When applying to the Panhellenes for inclusion, the Magnesians must have set out in detail not only their early wanderings and eventual settlement, but the help which they had given to other Greeks who had arrived on the soil of Asia. No less important were the benefactions which they had received from the Roman people in republican times, and from Hadrian in the imperial age.

The Panhellenion was not the only body that served this function of validating the claims of Asian cities to a Hellenic pedigree. Another was the "League of the Concord of the Greeks," a body based at Plataea in Boeotia, whose function was to commemorate the victory over the Persians in 479. Approximately in the reign of Hadrian, a certain Claudius Attalus from Synnada in Phrygia served as head of this body, and also as chief magistrate at Athens. In Sparta, he dedicated a statue of Athena in her guise as the civic goddess *(Polias)* of Synnada, proudly recalling that his city had been founded by a Spartan hero. Ever since Synnada rose to prominence in the late republic, it had taken pride in its mythic connections with both Athens and Sparta, and Attalus thus reaffirmed the links between his native city and the two protagonists of fifth-century Greece.[45]

In the Hellenistic age, the work of historians and poets, some of whom also served as ambassadors, had supplied the material for these diplomatic claims. The same continued to be true in the high empire, though it is a mark of the times that the same élite which formed the political classes often also supplied the speakers and writers engaged in the business of civic glorification. At Pergamum, a certain Claudius Charax was long known from literature as a historian who wrote a history of Greece and Rome. An epigram, probably inscribed on the title page, celebrated his city's mythic past: "I am Charax the priest, from the majestic height of Pergamum, where once against Achilles sacker of cities fought Telephus, blameless son of blameless Heracles." Modern discoveries have shown that Charax had a public career which exactly paralleled the dual interest of his history. He was both a generous benefactor of his city, in which he built the entrance-gate *(propylon)* to the great sanctuary of Asclepius, and a Roman consul in the year 147.[46] Charax can be seen as the last in a long line of Greek prose writers who combined myth, geography, and history.

By contrast with prose, mythological and especially epic poetry experienced a renewal. Two poets who were to be of high repute in later centuries were a father and son from Laranda, the "mother city" of Lycaonia in central Asia Minor. The father, Nestor, was honored in many cities of the empire, from Paphos in Cyprus to Rome itself. His son, Pisander, composed the longest poem known from antiquity, *The Marriages of Heroes and Gods* in sixty books. This "began with the marriage of Zeus and Hera, and brought all stories which occurred in the intervening ages down to his own day." A fragment of the work shows that he narrated a myth which linked his native Lycaonia to Arcadia in the Peloponnese. In this story, the Arcadian hero Lycaon was told by Apollo to found a city on the spot where he saw a wolf with a human hand in its jaws. It happens that the same myth is illustrated on coins of Laranda struck in the poet's lifetime.[47]

Like his father, Pisander must have traveled throughout the Roman empire, reciting appropriate portions of his poem, bringing renown to his hitherto obscure city, and affirming the link between the age of myth and his own time. He is a precursor of late antiquity—the epoch when Hellenism served simultaneously to reaffirm Greek culture and to form a bridge to the new culture of Christianity.

It happens that the only coin issues which explicitly advertise kinship *(syngeneia)* are roughly from the lifetime of Pisander. Struck at Attaleia in Pamphylia, they advertise its kinship with Athens and with Pisa, the site of the Olympic games. Behind this issue appears to lie a privilege granted to Attaleia by the emperor Valerian, the right to hold its own "sacred" Olympics. As a foundation of Pergamum, the city may well have had some claim to kinship with cities of mainland Greece, of which several of the Pergamene kings had been benefactors, but the particular myths are unknown. Cities of the Greek world still cultivated their mutual links and the favor of Roman emperors, though kinship diplomacy was now entering its last stage.[48]

IO

LATE ANTIQUITY

*T*here is only a slow transition from the imperial period to late antiquity. Many of the features of the later age are already present in the earlier, while some survive which might be thought to have perished in the disruptions of the third century. In particular, the life of the Greek *polis,* even if no longer expressed in inscribed laws, decrees, or dedications, persisted in a form which gave notable prominence to benefactors—more usually government officials than local gentry. The era might seem at first glance to be inhospitable for a diplomacy based on mythical and historical kinship. The "gods and heroes" so often invoked in the past were now discredited as demons, and "Hellene" no longer had its Herodotean sense of unity "in blood and language," but rather of adherence to a discredited culture and belief-system.[1]

Although the Christian apologists of the second century were radically hostile toward this new kind of Hellenism, by the fourth century the situation had become more nuanced, now that Christianity no longer had to fight for attention, and church fathers could ponder at leisure the place which classical learning should have in the education of the young.[2] Just as the major cities retained their vitality, though in different forms, so in many areas of public life, including those in which diplomacy was most at home, a training in classical culture was indispensable. A city honoring a governor with a statue and its accompanying epigram praised him for his "judgments equal to [those of] Themis, [the daughter] of Zeus," and yet this same governor conducted correspondence with saints.[3] As late as the reign of Justinian, the Christian rhetor Choricius of Gaza praised his equally Christian teacher, Procopius, deploying a medley of Greek and Christian learning which was to scandalize a Byzantine prelate.[4]

Diplomacy at the city level, even in the attenuated form of the high empire, is now rarely attested. The two treatises which survive under the name of Menander the Rhetor presuppose considerable activity on the part of local speakers, but little interaction between cities. The "ambassadorial" speech *(presbeutikos)* is now one addressed by a single speaker to a governor on behalf of a city in distress, an evolution aided by a shift in the sense of the word "embassy" *(presbeia)* to the meaning of "entreaty," "intercession." The "speech of invitation" *(klētikos)* is similarly aimed at luring an official to a local festival.[5] But since these two treatises continued to be read and copied in later ages, despite their overt paganism, they must have continued to fill a need. It was not so much the actual practice of diplomacy that had changed, as the ways of recording it. An example which happens to survive is an epigram on stone recording how the city of Aphrodisias, "the Mother of Caria," received from a city calling itself the "Mother of Phrygia" the gift of a statue of a high official, probably the vicar of Asiana. The balanced phrases suggest that the actual gift was accompanied by a ceremony in which the rights and traditions of the two cities were duly rehearsed. As is characteristic of late antiquity, however, only the epigram honoring the official survives to commemorate the transaction.[6]

A speech delivered in the era of Menander, on the eve of Constantine's conversion to Christianity, shows that appeals to kinship might still be used, though here it is kinship between his city and the emperor that the orator seeks to establish.[7] In 311 a nameless ambassador from Autun (Augustodunum) came before

Constantine, probably at Trier. His main task was to thank the emperor for a kindness (beneficium) granted a few years before, when he had granted Autun a remission of taxes and thus saved it from ruin. According to the speaker, this generosity was due to the city's position as the capital of the Aedui, whom the Roman people had long ago proclaimed as its "brothers." "These were the first of all, among the monstrous and barbaric tribes of Gaul, to be declared 'brothers of the Roman people' by many decrees of the senate. When not even peace, except a doubtful one, could be expected from the other people between Rhone and Rhine, the Aedui alone gloried in the name of kinship."[8] The orator recalls how other peoples had led Rome into troublesome wars by claims of "mythic origin" (fabulosa origo), for example the Mamertines of Sicily and the citizens of Ilium—the speaker is thinking of the First Punic War and of the war with Antiochus, though it is tendentious to blame the Ilians for the second. By contrast, an Aeduan ambassador from long ago, a chieftain "leaning on his shield," had persuaded the senate to give his people help against the Germans, and thus brought about Julius Caesar's invasion of Gaul.[9] By dismissing mythic kinships, the speaker wishes to represent the embassy to the republican senate as something more concrete, a matter of elective affinity rather than a vague and mischievous appeal to forgotten obligations.

A similar procedure, the appeal to kinship as expressed in verifiable history, appears in an orator and philosopher who illustrates the ambiguous role of Hellenic culture under Christian emperors. A lifelong pagan, Themistius enjoyed the trust of all the emperors from Constantine's son and successor, Constantius II, down to Theodosius I.[10] Two of his speeches, both of them addressed to Constantius, make play with terms of Greek diplomacy which go back to the classical era, "author" (archēgetēs), "kinsman" (syngenēs), "brother" (adelphos), endowing them with new meaning in a new age.

The first speech, slightly earlier in date, appears to have been delivered in the senate of Constantinople, though it celebrates the consulship which the emperor assumed in Milan in 357.[11] Like the orator of Menander's "invitation speech," Themistius is concerned to draw the emperor's favorable attention toward the capital, which he has rarely visited. Constantinople is a "temple" (*naos*) of the emperor, and owes its existence to his father Constantine. Thus the senate of Constantinople can also claim to be Constantine's creation, and so to be "of common father" (*homopatōr*) with Constantius. When the usurper Vetranio threatened Constantinople with destruction, he did so because he knew it to be "most dear and most akin [*oikeiotatē kai syngenestatē*] to the masters against whom he raged." [12] Here Themistius used the two adjectives which above all characterized the language of kinship diplomacy, *oikeios* and *syngenēs,* but now it is the relationship to the emperor that counts, not the relation between city and city. This development is already visible in the third century, for example in the correspondence between Decius and the city of Aphrodisias.

Later in the same year, Themistius went to Rome at the time when Constantius made his own first visit there, an occasion vividly described by Ammianus Marcellinus.[13] Speaking before the senate, he took the opportunity to rehearse the ties that bound the old Rome, the "mother city [*mētropolis*] of trophies," and the new. Quickly passing over the ancient services of Byzantium to Rome, he recalls the recent reign of the usurper Magnentius in Gaul, a period when Constantinople, alone "preserving a remnant of its father's family [*genos*]," sent Constantius to defeat the intruder. Thus Constantius has became a patriarch (*archēgetēs*) of Rome no less than Romulus, and the two Romes "gave each other reciprocal gifts, the one that was freed [Rome] giving the other a founder [Constantine], the one that was founded giving the other a savior [Constantius]." Later Themistius returns to a conceit which he used in his earlier speech, the idea of Constantinople as the emperor's sibling. Though Constantine founded the second capital, he died too soon to adorn it worthily. "Newly brought to the light of day from the pangs of labor, it had been left without its parent in need of clothing. But you took it up, as a loving elder brother takes up a tender little sister."[14]

Artificial as these ideas might appear, they show, in exactly the same way as the Gallic orator's panegyric of Constantine, the need to connect the speaker's city with the ruler, and to make it worthy of his attention. For this purpose, the old language of kinship had to be pressed into new forms, and it continued to be effective. In this same year of 357, Constantius established the senate of Constantinople as a body independent of Rome, giving Themistius the task of recruiting new members.[15] The "little sister" was well on its way to supplanting the ancient "mother city."

Themistius' friend and contemporary, Libanius of Antioch, was also a pagan, but much more conservative, and much less ready to transmute old forms into new. He was also more distant from the imperial court, except for one brief and intense period, the winter of 362–63, which his former pupil Julian, now emperor, spent in Antioch on his way to the ill-fated Persian expedition. Gravely offended by the conduct of the Antiochenes, the emperor threatened to spend the next winter in Tarsus of Cilicia. If carried out, the threat not only might have grave practical consequences, but it also struck the raw nerve of civic rivalry, no less sensitive in the fourth century than in the second or third. Libanius thereupon composed the only one of his speeches to be entitled "ambassadorial" *(presbeutikos)*, even though the emperor never in fact heard it. Like the "ambassadorial" speech recommended by Menander, it is a speech of intercession.[16] Libanius' argument could not be based on any actual kinship between the emperor and the city, not even an artificial one such as was devised by the orator of Autun or by Themistius. He could, however, claim a kinship of verbal culture *(syngeneia tou logou)* between the emperor and himself, based on his position as his former teacher. The idea that intellectual pursuits create a sort of kinship is already implied in Isocrates, but becomes explicit in the Hellenistic period.[17] As another kinsman *(syngenēs)* in the same spiritual family, Libanius appealed to his pupil Celsus, whom the emperor had recently appointed to be governor of Cilicia.[18]

Another speech of Libanius constitutes one of the most vivid documents of civic memory to survive from antiquity, his famous

Antiochene oration.[19] Based on local histories *(syngraphai),* his account perfectly exemplifies the Greek understanding of mythic and historic time as an indivisible continuity, even in this later phase of Hellenism. Layer by layer, the orator builds up his city's past from the time of the Argive Inachus, the son of Earth, who sent out a band of his subjects in search of his daughter Io. In a variation of the normal scheme, these are diverted from their mission and, reaching the land which was later to be the territory of Antioch, fall under its spell and decide to stay. Hereafter Libanius adds further colonists from Crete, Cyprus, and Elis, and then passes without a break to historical settlers—the Persians, Macedonians, and Romans. The underlying theme of this section is nobility *(eugeneia),* the same ideal that was pursued by cities of the high empire eager to find links with old Greece. That search was not incompatible with the recollection of favors from Macedon or Rome, though it is characteristic of Syrian and Phoenician cities rather than of ones of Asia Minor to recall these links in their official titles.[20]

Libanius shows that, by contrast with the rarefied or artificial kinships devised by a Themistius or a Julian, at the civic level the old traditions of descent and kinship persisted. In the late 350s, when Julian was as yet a professing Christian, a governor of Caria called Eros Monaxius endowed the city of Aphrodisias with a massive gate, still standing to the northwest of the ruins.[21] The inscription calls him a former Cretarch (high priest of the imperial cult in Crete), and speaks of the Aphrodisians as "kinsmen" *(syngeneis)* of the Cretans. Eros is almost certainly the official of this name who received a letter from Libanius:[22]

How worthy is your station of your toils and your culture [*logoi*]! Passing from the temples of the Muses [the world of culture] to the council, you began to excel and to display the orator in you. From the council you have come to office, and Justice shares your seat. As we therefore remember you and pray for you, you for your part must remember your ancestor Minos. Or rather, you do continue to remember him, and hence all is as it should be, when good fortune leads to success, and we can say what we always wished to say about you.

From the courtly phrases it emerges that Eros is a Cretan of the purest stock, descended from the mythical king and sea-lord, Minos. Such claims of heroic descent are attested among not only pagans but also Christians of the late empire, and bishops sometimes bear names which recall the mythology of their native cities.[23] This descent seems to have been a primary motive for Eros' generosity toward Aphrodisias, which like other cities of Caria had long claimed a kinship with Crete. There is a piquant contrast between this well-placed Cretan aristocrat and an Aphrodisian who portrayed Minos on his tomb some four centuries before, Augustus' freedman Zoilus. The mythic links that helped Aphrodisias in the fourth century now depended on courtiers and governors.[24]

This is the last inscribed text to refer to such public kinship, though less well preserved cities like Antioch or Constantinople may well have set up similar ones. Aphrodisias is also the last city to preserve a monument which, if not necessarily the result of diplomacy, nevertheless expresses the mythic origins on which such diplomacy fed, a sculptural counterpart to Libanius' *Antiochene Oration*. A relief perhaps to be dated to the fourth century, and set up in a large public building of the city, shows a series of mythological figures and scenes. The central figures are Ninus and Semiramis, both of whom occur in legends of the city's foundation. The appearance of Bellerophon and Pegasus (see Figure 4), though it recalls the speech of Glaucus in the *Iliad*, integrates them into the mythic past of Aphrodisias, which counted Bellerophon among its founders.[25]

The tradition of civic encomia on which Libanius draws in his *Antiochene* oration also lies behind a characteristic literary genre of late antiquity, the so-called *patria*, monographs devoted to the monuments of ancient cities and their attendant myths and histories.[26] These works, and the many local histories that lay behind

Figure 4. Fourth-century relief of Aphrodisias (Caria), showing Pegasus and Bellerophon

them, in turn nourished the last epic of classical antiquity (even if probably written by a Christian), Nonnus' *Dionysiaca*. The poet's home city of Panopolis, situated in the Egyptian Thebaid, is the Greek descendant of the Egyptian Chemmis, the very place in which Herodotus learned about Perseus recognizing his long-lost relatives *(syngeneis)*. His poem preserves not only the memory of heroic founders, such as Byzas at Byzantium and Perseus at Tarsus, but also seems to echo current rivalries between cities such as Tyre and Beirut.[27] When he places the birth of Byzas in Egypt rather than in the city of which he was the eponym, the poet is embroidering the tradition in order to make his native country the origin of the New Rome.[28]

About two generations after Nonnus, under Justinian I, the scribe Stephanus of Byzantium compiled an alphabetical index of cities and the epithets derived from them, with plentiful citation of long-past authorities on their myths and history, though his work now survives only in a pitiful abridgment. It has been understood as a guidebook for the officials and scribes of the resurgent empire, a source on which they could draw when corresponding with governors or foreign potentates. Just as the artifacts of Byzantium teem with figures of classical mythology, so (it appears) did cities still take pride in their mythic past, with no feeling that it compromised their faith.[29]

The reign of Justinian provides a curious last instance of a ruler moved to generosity by considerations of mythic kinship. An imperial directive of the year 535 is addressed to the powerful John of Cappadocia, praetorian prefect of the East, and concerns the region of Lycaonia in central Asia Minor, in which Justinian had decided to combine the civil and military authority under a single governor, or praetor: "We considered it right to adorn the province of the Lycaonians with greater honor than it now has, considering its earliest beginnings, such as they are handed down to us by those who have written and recorded ancient matters, and considering also that it is very closely akin [*syngenestaton*] to the Romans, and founded almost from the same causes."[30] As the emperor proceeds to explain, long before the time of Aeneas the eponymous Lycaon began his career as an Arcadian king, but later settled in Italy, where his conquests inaugurated the Roman empire. From Italy he sent out a colony to Lycaonia, naming the region after himself, and the emperor considers this a sufficient reason to "adorn it with the ancient emblems of Roman dignity." This tradition contains elements of kinship myth in their purest form—the hero who wanders to another country, the king who sends out colonists to distant lands—and it may well owe its vitality to Pisander of Laranda, the prolific poet of the third century. John of Cappadocia, whose native region was linked to Lycaonia by geography and history, presumably did not need to be told these details. Rather, he must have requested Justinian to bestow this privilege upon the Lycaonians. It would be a final act of kinship diplomacy, conducted in the true late antique fashion between a minister and his king.

Conclusion

THE HUMAN AND
OTHER FAMILIES

*D*iplomatic appeals to kinship between states, whether as small as the average *polis* or as large as the Roman empire, existed through most of antiquity, and the permutations of such kinship diplomacy can serve as a platform from which to view political changes in the Graeco-Roman world. Of these the most salient is the rise of Rome to the status of a world power. Second only in importance is perhaps the rise of Christianity, with its competing vision of kinship within the church.

How effective was kinship diplomacy? Was it "artificial" at least in the later stages of its existence, as has sometimes been held? Did it have any important effect in real life, so as for example to turn the scale between life and death for persons or individuals? The concept of artificiality is not really helpful, since such kinships, being extensions of familial relations, were always constructions. If "artificial" means "invented for the purpose of deception," certainly kinship diplomacy uses fictitious documents or arguments, such as the decree of the Cretans supporting the foundation of Magnesia on the Maeander. It is not proven, however, that these were known to the Magnesians as inventions, rather than being borrowed from sources such as local historians.

There is perhaps no known case in which ambassadors cite documents with the intent to deceive. In this respect, ancient diplomacy compares favorably with that of later ages, when documents such as the Donations of Constantine or the Protocol of the Elders of Zion have been used by powers who knew they were fraudulent.

The charge of ineffectiveness is more difficult to answer, for the reason that arguments from kinship often formed part of a bundle which included other ones such as military advantage. Thus Aristagoras of Miletus, when addressing the Spartans and Athenians, appealed not only to the kinship of Ionians with the motherland, but also to the advantages which the two cities would gain from the expedition.[1] Even when a historical agent ascribed his own actions to considerations of kinship, as Antiochus III "dedicated" Xanthus to his ancestor Apollo, he may have intended to put an appearance of morality on a material calculation, such as the need to save his effective strength for more important objectives. Nonetheless, the choice of cover is still significant. Even for the most calculating of autocrats, the appearance of respect for outward forms can be of practical advantage.

If such respect was indeed advantageous, then the question arises: from what sources did kinship diplomacy derive its strength? In its origins, it takes Greek concepts of the household, the family, and the clan, and applies them to dealings between communities. These might in fact share such links in historical time, as a mother city did with its colonies, but sometimes they had to find their links in the mythic past and then "renew" them. The essential Greekness of such diplomacy is a large part of its success. The attractive power of Greek culture, whether embodied in epic poetry or in concrete productions of metalwork and ceramics, is manifest from the archaic period on among foreign peoples such as the Persians, the Etruscans, and the Lycians. The Persian use of Ionian craftsmen, for example, is already seen in the buildings of Cyrus the Great,[2] and the royal tombs of Vergina are dazzling monuments to the strength of Greek culture in late fourth-century Macedon. Lycian princes of the Xanthus valley were eager to see their country associated with the fall of Troy, just as Etruscan ones treasured vases which showed Aeneas fleeing from Troy to begin his journey to the West.

For the Greeks, usually organized in their characteristic unit of the *polis,* and often confronted with larger powers, kinship diplomacy offered a way to negotiate not only within the family but also outside it, in the realm of "philhellenes" and even "barbarians." It may well be untrue that Xerxes appealed to the Argives to stay neutral in his invasion of Greece. But Herodotus, who has doubts about this incident, is less incredulous about another, that soon after Xerxes' death Argive ambassadors arrived at the Persian court to renew the friendship between the two states.[3] Troy, now renamed Ilium, enjoyed a period of prosperity in the early Hellenistic period, and then went into a decline. It was revived first by Antiochus III as part of his campaign to reaffirm Seleucid rule in western Asia, and even more by the Romans, for whom magnanimity and generosity to the weak contributed to their national self-image. "The greatness of the empire of the Romans," so one of them held, "is shown not by what they take, but by what they bestow."[4] The advantages of a connection, by birth or "familiarity," with these western newcomers were incalculable. As Ilium owed its rebirth to the Romans, so Aphrodisias in Caria owed them its existence as a city.

Granting the effectiveness of kinship diplomacy, though that effectiveness is rarely as visible as in the case of Ilium or Aphrodisias, raises the further question of its evolution and eventual demise. While Greek in its language and forms, it has both a Greek and a Roman phase, as indeed does all of what is often called "classical antiquity" or "the ancient world." It clearly enters a new phase with the arrival of the Romans on the world scene, when it no longer serves to protect the city against the threat of extinction, but rather to promote it in competition with others within the Roman system. In the imperial period, it reflects the increasing domination of power by individuals, in the first place the emperors and their immediate families and favorites, secondarily the wealthy benefactors and local aristocrats on whom Rome depended for its control of the cities. With the decline of the city in late antiquity, or rather with the growth of administrative machinery, only those individuals in contact with the central power, a Themistius or a John of Cappadocia, are in a position to obtain and confer the benefactions which once lay within the power of city magnates such as Herodes Atticus of Athens or Opramoas of Rhodiapolis in Lycia.

Kinship diplomacy thus withered in the Roman imperial period, partly because it was displaced by other forms of negotiation, especially private influence with those in power. In addition, *syngeneia,* the connection created by the common ancestor of two descent-groups, was essentially a Greek concept, which the Romans acknowledged though it corresponded only in part to their own notions of clan *(gens).* In addition, Roman diplomacy had its own forms and language, which were not always easily translated into Greek, for example the term *amicitia* (friendship), with its connotations often far removed from Greek *philia.*[5]

Even in Greek, moreover, the term *genos* had begun at least as early as the fourth century to denote "kind" or "type," without reference to birth. Hence Isocrates can claim that his native Athens has caused the word "Hellenes" to denote intellect and not descent, a share in Athenian culture rather than the "joint birth" of all Greeks.[6] From here it was a short step to the idea that community of culture is a stronger bond than community of birth. Echoing Isocrates' claim five centuries later, Aelius Aristides told his Roman listeners, "It is not by a proud refusal to give anybody a share in your city that you have made it admirable. You sought a worthy population for it, and you have brought it about that the name of 'Roman' designates a kind of common family [*genos*], not one family among the others either, but one equal to all the rest."[7] What Rome extended, however, was the membership in the political class of Roman citizens, and this was always dependent on the generosity of the imperial donor, and revocable at his will.[8]

By a similar evolution, the adjective *eugenēs,* "well-born," "noble," and its abstract *eugeneia,* like "noble" and "gentle" in English, began already in the classical period to denote moral excellence, and not only the excellence conferred by Greek origins. In the latter sense it continued to be applied to communities or persons with long, usually Greek ancestry. But just as Aristides can use *genos* of all Roman citizens, so the emperor Justinian can talk of Caracalla admitting all into "Roman nobility" *(Rōmaikē eugeneia)* by his general grant of the citizenship.

Other, competing notions of descent and kinship were to have profounder effects, and to spell the end of kinship diplomacy in its classical form. The early Stoics had long since preached the idea of Zeus as the common father.[9] The first historian of Christianity, the Hellenized Luke, describes Paul of Tarsus citing the formulation of this idea by "one of your own poets" to the Athenian Areopagus, "for we are of his race" *(genos)*. This speech of Paul, which represents kinship diplomacy transposed into a new key, may not be historical, but it announces a world in which all mankind, especially all who have heard the Christian "good news," are of one family, and "Hellenes" are those who have refused their assent, the "nations" *(ethnē)*, "pagans."[10] Outside observers marveled at the Christians' extension of the term "brother," or at their concept of spiritual "children." In due course, these Christian ideas were to foster new and powerful institutions such as the church-made relationship between natural and god-parents, *synteknia*, "sharing of children." There is a palpable contrast with *syngeneia*, sharing of descent-group.[11]

The idea that the simple condition of being human, "humanity" in its most basic sense, involves entering into a family, and into certain rights and responsibilities, is already audible in the speech of Glaucus the Lycian in the sixth book of the *Iliad*. Thereafter this idea exists alongside that of a more particular kinship, determined by immediate kin, by descent from a common eponym or "originator" *(archēgetēs)*, by links of migration or colonization. Since such particularism is paradoxically part of the fabric of human nature, "ties of mutual kindred," overt or covert, are likely to endure, enjoying lesser or greater importance, so long as human beings continue to practice diplomacy.

Appendixes
Abbreviations
Notes
Select Bibliography
Index

Appendix I

LEGENDS OF GREECE
AND CARIA

$\mathcal{T}$he longest of all inscriptions involving the diplomacy of kinship is the great stele from Xanthus of Lycia which records an embassy from the Cytenians, "Dorians of the metropolis."[1] The Xanthian decree which takes up most of the text recounts in detail the mythological arguments employed by the Dorian ambassadors. In this section of the decree, one part requires more elucidation than it has received so far. This runs: "Aletes, who was one of the Heraclidae, came to the aid of those who had been sent from our land [Xanthus] as colonists by Chrysaor, the son of Glaucus and son of Hippolochus; for he [Aletes], starting from the Dorian land, helped them when they were being warred upon, and after ending the danger that beset them he married the daughter of Aor, son of Chrysaor."[2]

In the segment rendered above as "sent from our land as colonists by Chrysaor," the Greek is τῶν ἀποικισθέντων ἐκ τῆς ἡμετέρας ὑπὸ Χρυσάορος. The first editor, Jean Bousquet, understands it differently:

Errant, comme fut son père, Alétès descendait la vallée du Céphise, en venant de Doride, lorsqu'il tomba sur une caravane d'émigrants qui la remontaient, avec leurs chariots bâchés, et se défendaient contre une attaque, j'allais dire d'Indiens (βοηθῆσαι πολεμουμένοις). Le cavalier solitaire vint à leur secours et les délivra du danger (τὸν περιεστηκότα κίνδυνον λύσαντα). Enfin, pour achever la ressemblance avec le folklore du Nouveau Monde, il épouse la petite-fille du chef de la caravane: συνοικῆσαι τὴν Ἄορος τοῦ Χρυσάορος θυγατέρα.[3]

Amusing as it is, this interpretation does not quite do justice to the Greek. First, the verb ἀποικίζω, when it has a personal object, means "send away from home," "send to a new home," not "lead out."[4] A passage of Xenophon's *Oeconomicus* concerning the life of bees is revealing: when the young are ready for work, the queen "sends them out to found a colony with someone to lead the new generation," ἀποικίζει αὐτοὺς σὺν τῶν ἐπιγόνων τινὶ ἡγεμόνι.[5] Hence it was not Chrysaor who led the group of settlers but someone else, whom the context shows to be his son Aor. The pattern whereby colonizing kings employ their sons to lead colonists recurs for example in Herodotus' account of the settlement of Etruria (Tyrrhenia) by Tyrsenus, the son of the Lydian king Atys.[6] The notion of a regular colony, not merely a caravan, is also suggested by the passive participle πολεμουμένοις, which is consistent with a formal war. Lastly, the verb ὁρμηθέντα, "setting out from," again suggests not a solitary traveler but a leader at the head of troops and with a fixed base.[7]

Aletes is well placed to play the role of such a leader, since he is celebrated in Greek mythology as the first Dorian king of Corinth, which he captured with the help of numerous allies at a time when it was ruled by kings descended from Sisyphus the son of Aeolus.[8] Pausanias, the excellence of whose information is once again corroborated by the new text, gives this account: "The Dorians made an expedition against Corinth, under the leadership of Aletes the son of Hippotas . . . Doridas and Hyanthidas [the reigning Sisyphids] yielded the throne to Aletes but remained there, while the common people of Corinth were driven out by the Dorians after losing to them in battle."[9] The Xanthian text might imply that Aletes had already left his Dorian homeland for good when he came across Aor and his fellow settlers, but the Greek might suggest that he was still based in Doris.

By contrast, Aor was hitherto unknown. His father's filiation, however, "son of Glaucus son of Hippolochus," shows that he must be a grandson of the Glaucus who confronts Diomedes so memorably in the sixth book of the *Iliad*. Since the return of the Heraclidae was conventionally placed three generations after the Trojan War, a grandson of the Homeric Glaucus would fit comfortably as a senior ally of Aletes. The pattern whereby a prince from abroad marries the daughter of a local chieftain is another known from myth, conspicuously in Vergil's *Aeneid*.

Though Aor himself was unknown, his name can now be recognized in a controversial document. This is a decree discovered on Delos in 1908, and first published by Louis Robert forty years later. Issued by a Doric-speaking city about 300, it honors two Athenians named Xenocles and Pausimachus (the second of these belonged to a family which was still prominent in the second century before our era). Though Robert noticed certain features of the document which might suggest Corinth, he opted for Phlius, Corinth's neighbor to the southwest, in part because the city issuing the decree had a tribe whose members were called "Aoreis," and Phlius was known to have had a mythical hero called "Aoris," son of the first founder, Aras. Corinth, however, was not known in 1948 to have had any hero of the name. That was still true in 1960, when Robert returned to the question, continuing to defend his first proposal, but not without serious consideration of the claims of Corinth. Then, in 1980, Nicholas Jones argued strongly for Corinth as the city, citing among other considerations the fact that Corcyra, a colony of Corinth, had a phyle called perhaps "Aworoi" (᾽ΑϜοροί), and his views have been widely but not universally accepted. The matter is presumably settled by the revelation that Aletes was married to the daughter of a certain Aor, all the more since a late tradition says that he created the original eight tribes of Corinth.[10]

Whether Aletes or some later ruler named the tribes of Corinth, he can hardly have been thinking of Lycia, which does not
begin to show traces of Hellenism before the sixth century. The
Dorian ambassadors, however, doubtless expert in the lore of
their kinsmen the Corinthians, must at least have known of a link
between Aletes and an Aor of central Greece. Here yet another
tradition preserved by Pausanias may be relevant. "Besides
Glaucus, the father of Bellerophon, Sisyphus had another son,
Ornytion . . . Ornytion's son was Phocus, nominally the son
of Poseidon. He migrated to Tithorea, in what is now called
Phocis."[11] Phocis would have been in the path of a band moving
southeast from Doris toward the Peloponnese, and conceivably
the Dorian ambassadors knew of some Aor, or some tradition of
Xanthian colonization, in this region which took its name from
Phocus the Sisyphid.

As Bousquet notes, Stephanus of Byzantium knows of a colonizing Chrysaor, not a descendant of Bellerophon but his brother.
The mutilated remains of Stephanus' *Ethnica* contain the following entry for the Carian city of Mylasa: "[Named after] Mylasus,
the son of Chrysaor, the son of Glaucus, the son of Sisyphus, the
son of Aeolus."[12] Chrysaor appears again as the father of Idrieus,
who allegedly give his name to "Idrias," the city later called
"Europus." Here Stephanus' source is Apollonius in his *Carian
History,* that is, the historian of unknown date from Aphrodisias.[13]
Another entry in Stephanus, now badly mutilated, also goes back
to Apollonius, and seems to refer to this Chrysaor as a colonizer:
"Chrysaoris, a city of Caria later called 'Idrias.' Apollonius in the
seventh book of his *Carian History:* 'And the first city of those
founded by the Lycians . . .' The ethnic name is 'Chrysaoris,' as
the same author [testifies] in the same work, 'The Tauropolitae
<and the Chrysaorians> and the Plarasians were allies.' There is
also a deme [called] 'Chrysaoris.' Epaphroditus says that all Caria
was called 'Chrysaoris.'"[14]

Stephanus' references clearly reflect the existence of the
Chrysaorian League, a Carian confederation called by Strabo the
Χρυσαορικὸν σύστημα. This was probably founded in the third

quarter of the third century, and had its heartland in the valley of the Marsyas (the modern Çine Çay). Bousquet infers that the Dorian ambassadors had visited one or more of the cities of the league, and he may well be right. However, the Chrysaor whom the Xanthians recognize in this decree seems to be, not a putative brother of Bellerophon (who has many links with Caria), but a later one, who lived about a generation before the return of the Heraclidae. Xanthus no doubt had mythical connections to many cities, and the complexity and variety of their traditions should not be underestimated.[15]

Stephanus' references to the earlier Chrysaor are drawn from the *Carian History* of Apollonius of Aphrodisias. There is no sign that this city was ever in the Chrysaorian League, but evidence is accumulating which links it with legends of Bellerophon, Pegasus, and one of the several Chrysaors. Aphrodisian coins of the early third century of our era depict Pegasus. The name "Chrysaor" (with the by-forms "Chrysaoris" and "Chrysaorius," the latter borne by a Christian bishop) is attested there. A newly discovered statue-base of imperial date bore a likeness of Bellerophon as founder *(ktistēs)*. In addition, the so-called Ninus Frieze, a series of late-antique reliefs carved with legends of the city's foundation, contained a panel of Pegasus, Bellerophon, and oracular Apollo. (See Figure 4.) The god is probably represented in his role of *archēgetēs*, the "initiator" of colonies.[16] These legends must come from Plarasa, a Carian city commonly thought to have been on the site of Bingeç, some fifteen kilometers southwest of Aphrodisias. When Aphrodisias was founded in the second century, it was joined with Plarasa in a community of joint citizenship *(sympoliteia)*. In due course it absorbed the older city, and in such situations the survivor often took over the myths of its predecessor.[17] Apollonius was thus in a position to know of an alliance between Plarasa, Chrysaoris, and "Tauropolis." This last city cannot be precisely located, but was presumably somewhere in the Taurus range.[18]

Appendix 2

LEGENDS OF LYCIA

*J*ust as the ambassadors of the Dorian metropolis instruct the Xanthians about traditions linking their land with Lycia, so also within Lycia does Hieron, an ambassador from Sidyma, link his native city with Tlos and other cities of the region. This transaction is known only from an inscription of imperial date, probably of the second century, whose interpretation has long proved difficult, but is now reasonably clear.[1]

In the version narrated by Hieron, the eponymous ancestor of the Termilai (the Lycians' name for themselves in their own language) was a certain Termiles, who had three sons, Tlous, Pinarus, and Cragus. The first was the eponym of Tlos in the Xanthus valley; the second had the same relation to Pinara, lying in a fold of the Cragus range on the valley's west side; while Cragus is presumably the eponym either of the same mountain range or of a city in the same area which no longer existed in historical times.[2] This story conforms to the pattern of three brothers who are the ancestors of three related cities or tribes, for example the three brothers Mysus, Lydus, and Car, respectively ancestors of the Mysians, Lydians, and Carians in Herodotus.[3]

As an authority for his version, Hieron cites one Polycharmus, a writer of uncertain date.[4] The tradition is, however, much older, for Stephanus of Byzantium, in the sixth century of our era, happens to preserve a "fragment" from the epic poet Panyassis of Halicarnassus in which several of the same names recur. This poet is roughly contemporary with Herodotus, and, according to some accounts, his relative. The only poem attributed to him is an epic on Heracles, the *Heracleis,* and this is usually taken to be the source of these lines.[5] They have been much studied, but some advance in their understanding is still possible.

The text given by the recent Teubner editor is as follows:

ἔνθα δ' ἔναιε μέγας Τρεμίλης καὶ ἔγημε θύγατρα
νύμφην Ὠγυγίην, ἣν Πραξιδίκην καλέουσιν,
Σίβρῃ ἐπ' ἀργυρέῃ ποταμῷ παρὰ δινήεντι·
τῆς δ' ὀλοοὶ παῖδες Τλῶος Ξάνθος Πίναρός τε
καὶ Κράγος, ὃς κρατέων πάσας ληίζετ' ἀρούρας.

Here lived the great Tremiles, and married his [?] daughter, the nymph Ogygie, whom they call Praxidike, by the silvery Sibrus, beside the whirling river. Her baneful sons were Tlous, Xanthus, Pinarus, and Cragus, who in his strength[?] ravaged all the fields.

It is not possible to discuss here all the problems raised by this text, but something may be said about the interpretation of lines 3 through 5, and the relevance of the fragment to the *Heracleis* from which it presumably comes.

In line 3, the "Sibrus" must be the river more usually called the Xanthus or "Yellow River," whose valley forms the heartland of the Lycian peninsula. This gave its name to Lycia's most important city, past which it flows shortly before reaching the sea, and in the region of the city it is conspicuously yellow to this day.[6] According to Strabo, the older name of the Xanthus was "Sirbis," while the twelfth-century scholar Eustathius gives the form "Sirmis."[7] Panyassis therefore parts company with Homer, who calls the river only by its Greek name. He also seems to making a learned point when using the epithet "silvery" for a stream which is in fact conspicuously yellow for most of its course. This may be simply may be a bow to his epic predecessor, who applies the epithet "silver-eddying" (ἀργυροδίνης) to the Xanthus in the Troad.[8] But Panyassis may refer to a remarkable natural feature of the Lycian river, which was noticed only in the last century.

In January 1842 a British vessel, H. M. *Beacon*, "visited the coast of Lycia . . . for the purpose of carrying away the remarkable remains of antiquity discovered by Sir Charles Fellows." This visit was later to be written up by two technicians attached to the expedition, the surveyor Thomas Spratt and the naturalist Edward Forbes. On their arrival they found the Xanthus "extremely rapid, and charged with pale yellow mud, derived from the tertiary clay, through which it has to run a great part of its course." The two explorers then journeyed up the valley in search of the river's source, and describe their discovery as follows:

> The next day we walked to the foot of the mountains, which here rise immediately from the plain to a height of eight thousand feet. Our object was to visit an enormous perpendicular precipice, at the foot of which the people throughout the valley assured us the Xanthus had its source. On arriving there, we found that there was, indeed, a great source of water, which, strange to say, seemed to gush out of the earth at the foot of an old tree . . . The Xanthus is born a full-grown river; for, at a few feet from its birth-place, it is a deep, boiling, and almost impassable torrent . . . At its source the Xanthus is clear and pure: it is not until it becomes charged with the mud from the tertiary banks through which it cuts a little lower down, that it assumes a dirty yellow hue.[9]

It seems to follow that Panyassis did not locate the marriage of Termiles and Praxidike vaguely by the Xanthus, but precisely at its source, where the two British travelers found it "clear and pure." The place where the river seemed to issue miraculously from the earth, at the foot of an enormous cliff, is suitable for the

union of the gigantic Termiles and the nymph Ogygie or Praxidike, and Panyassis' expression, "eddying river," corresponds exactly with the description by Spratt and Forbes, "a deep, boiling
torrent."

In the second hemistich of line 4, the current texts fail to reproduce the word order of the manuscripts, which give, not Τλῶος
ξανθὸς Πίναρός τε, but Τλῶος ξανθός τε Πίναρος. That the
latter order is right is shown by a discovery made at Xanthus itself, where an inscription of the early fourth century honors a local dynast called Arbinas. It is a poem written by a Greek from
Pellana in Achaea, and mentions among Arbinas' conquests
Ξάνθον τε ἠδὲ Πίναρα καὶ εὐλίμενον Τελ[εμεσσόν]. This
surely settles the question in favor of scanning Πίναρος with a
long alpha in Panyassis, and justifies the word order in the manuscripts of Stephanus.[10] That phrasing has the added advantage
of making the brothers in Panyassis three and not four, "Tlous,
fair-haired Pinarus, and Cragus," exactly as in the discourse of
Hieron.

The last line in Stephanus' quotation from Panyassis is concerned with Cragus, "who in his strength[?] was ravaging all the
fields." He must be another eponym, above all the eponym of
the formidable mountain which dominates the southern part of
the Xanthus valley on the west.[11] Although κρατέων, "in his
strength," may be sound, it is tempting to suppose that Panyassis is
again referring to an ancient tradition from the legendary history
of Lycia, that it was settled by immigrants from Crete. According
to Herodotus,

> The Lycians are originally from Crete, for originally all of
> Crete was inhabited by barbarians. But Minos and Sarpedon,
> the sons of Europa, quarreled over the kingship, and when
> Minos prevailed in the faction, he drove Sarpedon out and
> his followers as well. Thus expelled, they arrived in the re-
> gion of Asia called Milyas, this being the original name of the
> area now inhabited by the Lycians, while the Milyans were
> then called Solymoi. For a while Sarpedon ruled them, and

they had the name which the Lycians are still given by their neighbors, Termilai.[12]

Thus Herodotus too seems to envisage the native Lycians, named after Termiles, as having been ruled by Sarpedon and his followers from Crete. In the "fragment" of Panyassis, then, it may be proposed that a proper name has been corrupted (as was all the more likely to happen in an isolated quotation) and that the last line was originally:

καὶ Κράγος, ὃς Κρητῶν πάσας ληίζετ᾽ ἀρούρας.

If Panyassis made the settlers Cretans, he must already have mentioned their arrival in Lycia. And if he represented them as attacked by Cragus, son of the "great Termiles" and eponym of the formidable mountain to the west, then that might explain the context of these lines within his epic on Heracles—the hero came to the rescue of the beleaguered Cretans, much as Aletes came to the rescue of Aor and his colonists in Greece. That version would have contradicted the chronology of Homer, who puts Heracles a generation before the Trojan War, but the difficulty of accommodating the exploits of Sarpedon to one lifetime was already noticed in antiquity. Some mythographers accordingly made him live for three generations.[13]

Whether or not this emendation is accepted, it is certain that Panyassis' epic brought Heracles to Lycia, and here too the poet may well have followed local tradition. Beginning in the first half of the fifth century, which is also the period of Panyassis, several coins struck by Lycian dynasts represent Heracles. One such depiction on a coin of the dynast Kuprlli, struck about the middle of the fifth century and intended for circulation in the Xanthus valley, has drawn attention because of its unusual quality. It has been described as follows:

Heracles is depicted in an interesting and artistically outstanding manner. He fights forward to the left, resting his

Figure 5. Coin of Arbinas, dynast of Xanthus, Lycia,
showing Heracles with lionskin and foot on rock

whole weight on his bent right leg, while the left is stretched
backwards and only rests lightly on the ground. The right
arm holds the club up and back over the head. The left arm
is stretched backwards and down and holds an indetermin-
able object. The left leg, arm and club are almost parallel.
This feature, united with the great tenseness in the chest and
abdomen, creates a figure of exceptional strength and
drive.[14]

This type resembles one struck by the already mentioned Arbinas
in the early fourth century. (See Figure 5.) Here again is a numis-
matist's description:

Heracles moves towards the left and has just placed his bent,
left leg on a rock while supporting himself on the toes of his
right leg, the leg being slightly bent and the instep outstretched. He is clad only in the lion-skin lying over his head

and left arm with the paw hanging down to his left knee. His outstretched left arm holds the bow, which of is of ordinary not composite type. Hanging from a strap over the right shoulder he carries a scabbard containing a sword on his left hip. His uplifted right hand carries the club, the point directed backwards.[15]

Whatever the interpretation of these coins, they suggest that the Lycians had developed their own variants on the myth of Heracles by the time of Panyassis. The second coin in particular, with its depiction of a rock on which the hero leans, would suit a legend involving a struggle with Cragus, eponym of a formidable mountain.

ABBREVIATIONS

Abbreviations generally follow the style of *The Oxford Classical Dictionary*, 3rd edition, eds. S. Hornblower and A. J. S. Spawforth (1996). Some which differ from the *OCD*, or might be unfamiliar, are listed below.

BEFAR
Bibliothèque des Ecoles françaises d'Athènes et de Rome

Chantraine, *Dict. étym.*
P. Chantraine, *Dictionnaire étymologique de la langue grecque,* 4 vols. (Paris, 1968–1980)

Curty, *Parentés*
O. Curty, *Les parentés légendaires entre cités grecques* (Geneva, 1995)

IIlion
P. Frisch, *Die Inschriften von Ilion* (Bonn, 1975)

ILampsakos
P. Frisch, *Die Inschriften von Lampsakos* (Bonn, 1978)

IMagnesia
O. Kern, *Die Inschriften von Magnesia am Maeander* (Berlin, 1900)

IPergamon
M. Fränkel, *Altertümer von Pergamon* 8.1 and 2: *Die Inschriften von Pergamon* (Berlin, 1890–1895)

IPergamon (Asklep)
C. Habicht, *Altertümer von Pergamon* 8.3: *Die Inschriften des Asklepieions* (Berlin, 1969)

IPriene   H. von Gaertringen, *Inschriften von Priene*
                            (Berlin, 1906)

IStratonikeia   M. Çetin Şahin, *Die Inschriften von Stratonikeia,*
                            2 vols. (Bonn, 1981–1982)

PECS   R. Stillwell, ed., *The Princeton Encyclopedia of
                            Classical Sites* (Princeton, 1976)

Walbank, *HCP*   F. W. Walbank, *A Historical Commentary on
                            Polybius,* 3 vols. (Oxford, 1957–1978)

NOTES

For complete citations of most works mentioned in the notes, other than encyclopedia articles, see the Select Bibliography.

Introduction

1. J. M. Hall, *Ethnic Identity in Greek Antiquity* 5.
2. See now Hall, *Ethnic Identity*.
3. For a bibliography of recent studies, ibid., 41 n. 65.
4. For this reason, I think it an error of method to treat "parentés légendaires" as a special type, as O. Curty does in his otherwise admirable book (Curty, *Parentés*).

1. The Language of Kinship Diplomacy

1. On the Siboi, O. Wecker, *RE* 2 A (1923) 2069–70. For the Macedonian kings as "Temenidai," Thuc. 2.99.3, with S. Hornblower, *A Commentary on Thucydides* I 375. On myths of Heracles in India, P. A. Brunt, *Arrian: History of Alexander and Indica II* (Cambridge, Mass., 1983), app. XVI.
2. Diod. Sic. 17.96.2.
3. L. Robert, *Hellenica* 1 (1940) 96 n. 5.
4. Diod. Sic. 4.1.3 = *FGrH* 70 T 8.

5. M. P. Nilsson, *Cults, Myths, Oracles, and Politics in Ancient Greece* 12; cf. 14. Similarly, Brunt, *Arrian* I (Cambridge, Mass., 1976) 464: "In general the Greek world did not distinguish legend from history."

6. "Human generation": 3.122.2. Causes of the Persian Wars: 1.1–5. Talthybius: 7.134–137. Pheidippides: 6.105; cf. his comment on the sham Athene of Peisistratus, 1.60.3–5. Myth: 2.23, 2.45.1.

7. Thuc. 1.22.4, with the commentary of Gomme; cf. 1.21.1.

8. Minos: 1.4. Sitalces: 2.29.3 (see Chapter 3).

9. *Il.* 4.58 (Hera), 12.23 (race of half-divine men), 6.209–210 (Glaucus). The word *geneē*, though it has the additional sense of "persons living at the same time, generation," often seems to function merely as a metrically convenient synonym of *genos*. See H. Ebeling, *Lexicon Homericum* I (Leipzig, 1885); and M. Schmidt in *Lex. frühgr. Epos* s.v. γενέη, γένος.

10. Bibliography in J. K. Davies, *OCD*³ 630, though the discussion is confined largely to Athens.

11. Hdt. 7.134–37. On Temenus, C. Sourvinou-Inwood, *OCD*³ 1481.

12. Hdt. 1.56.3 (Dorus), 7.94 (Ion), 1.57 (the Attic *genos* changed its language on joining the Hellenes); Thuc. 1.3.2 (Hellenes). See also C. P. Jones, *CQ* 46 (1996) 315–320.

13. Eur. *Ion* 1581–94.

14. On this complex subject, D. Musti, *Ann. Scuol. Norm. Pisa* 32 (1963) 225–239; Curty, *Parentés;* in criticism of Curty, E. Will, *Rev. Phil.* 69 (1995) 299–325; J. M. Hall, *CR* 47 (1997) 96–98. Whereas Musti 238–239 holds that kinships become more "artificial" after the early Hellenistic period, I will argue rather that they assume a different kind of significance.

15. Thus Sall. *Jug.* 18.3 (Heracles' followers in Africa).

16. Persians: Hdt. 7.150. Aeneadae: D. L. Page, *Further Greek Epigrams* (Cambridge, 1981) 478; Bailey on Lucr. 1.1. Noah: Gen. 10:32. Abraham: Gen. 17:4, 6, 16. In general, E. J. Bickerman, *CP* 47 (1952) 65–81.

17. Tlepolemus: Pind. *Ol.* 7.78. Battus: *SEG* 9.3. 26 (Meiggs-Lewis 5). Apollo: Pind. *Pyth.* 5.60, etc. For the word *archēgetēs* in general, O. Jessen, *RE* 2 (1895) 441–444, esp. 441–442 on Apollo;

Chantraine, *Dict. étym.* s.v. ἄρχω B; I. Malkin, *Religion and Colonization in Ancient Greece* 241–250; Will, *Rev. Phil.* 69 (1995) 322–323.

18. Thuc. 1.24–55, esp. 1.25.4 and 1.34, on Corcyra's alleged neglect of its duty to Corinth as the "mother city." See A. J. Graham, *Colony and Mother-City in ancient Greece*[2] (Manchester, 1982) 10.

19. Cf. H. Bengtson, *Griechische Geschichte*[5] (Munich, 1977) 91–101 on the "second colonization," 457–458 on the "third and greatest epoch of colonization."

20. Thuc. 2.15.6; Rhodes on Aristot. *Const. Ath.* 8.4.

21. Hdt. 1.56.3; cf. 8.31; D. Rousset, *BCH* 113 (1989) 199–239.

22. Aristot. *Pol.* I 1252b.

23. *Syngeneia:* Thuc. 1.24.2. *Apogonoi:* Hdt. 7.150.2. *Mētropolis:* Thuc. 1.26.3.

24. Chantraine, *Dict. étym.* s.v. οἶκος B; for its use in Thucydides see now Hornblower, *Commentary on Thucydides* II 64–67; for its use in diplomacy, Curty, *Parentés* 224–241, generally understanding it as "un lien sans consanguinité."

25. E.g., Hdt. 3.65.5, 4.65.2.

26. Dover on Pl. *Symp.* 192 C 1: "a relationship in which one treats another with the affection appropriate to dealings with one's own kin."

27. Hdt. 1.94; cf. 1.7.3. For the argument that this is a Lydian fabrication of the sixth century, D. Briquel, *L'origine lydienne des Etrusques* (Rome, 1991).

28. For "Hellen," W. Süss, *RE* 8 (1912) 170–173; there appears to be no iconography (not in *LIMC*). On "Hellenes," W. Will, "Hellenen," *RAC* 14 (1988) 376–384; E. Hall, *Inventing the Barbarian* 3–8.

29. LSJ s.v. γένος, V.

30. Homer on Carians: *Il.* 2.867. The parallel with Russian *nemet'*, "dumb," and *Nemets*, "German," has often been drawn.

31. Hdt. 2.158.5 (cf. also 7.35.2, the "barbaric and presumptuous" words of Xerxes); Thuc. 7.29.4, 8.98.1.

32. For the term *philhellēn*, J.-L. Ferrary, *Philhellénisme et impérialisme* 497–504; idem in *Filellenismo e tradizionalismo a Roma* (Rome, 1996) 183–189. On Alexander I, N. G. L. Hammond, G. T.

Griffith, and F. W. Walbank, *A History of Macedonia* II 98–104. On Herodotus' presentation of him, R. Scaife, *Hermes* 117 (1989) 129–137; E. Badian in S. Hornblower, ed., *Greek Historiography* (Oxford, 1994) 107–130.

33. Hdt. 5.22 (Alexander); *SEG* 29.652 (tripod).

2. The Beginnings

1. LSJ cites Cic. *Att.* 10.17.4, *Fam.* 6.12.3 for the first uses.
2. For late Bronze Age evidence and examples, R. Payton, *Anat. Stud.* 41 (1991) 99–106 (the Ulu Burun diptych); D. Symington, ibid. 111–123; for Graeco-Roman antiquity, G. Lafaye in Dar.-Sag. V 1–3. For Roman military *diplomata* (though the term does not seem to be attested for them), T. Mommsen, *CIL* 3.2 (1873) 902–904. For the related phenomenon of "double documents" on papyrus, N. Lewis in *The Documents from the Bar-Kokhba Period in the Cave of Letters: Greek Papyri* (Jerusalem, 1989) 6–10.
3. *Oxford English Dictionary* s.v. "diplomacy" I.1, followed by H. G. Nicolson, *Diplomacy*[2] 15. For antiquity, D. Kienast, *RE* Suppl. 13 (1973) 499–628, is a useful repertoire. F. E. Adcock and D. J. Mosley, *Diplomacy in Ancient Greece* (London, 1975), discuss mainly the classical period.
4. Iris: for an overview of the relevant passages, H. Stadler, *RE* 9 (1916) 2038–39. Oneiros: *Il.* 2.5–34. Hermes in *Il.* 24 is sent by Zeus to Priam as a protector, not a messenger: MacLeod on *Il.* 24.334–335.
5. Chantraine, *Dict. étym.* s.v. ἄγγαρος, ἄγγελος; E. Risch in *Lex. frühgr. Epos* s.v. ἄγγελος.
6. *Il.* 1.321, 334.
7. Chantraine, *Dict. étym.* s.v. κῆρυξ; B. Mader in *Lex. frühgr. Epos* s.v. κῆρυξ.
8. *Il.* 3.203–224, 11.138–142.
9. *Il.* 9.162–713. Heralds: 9.170.
10. *Il.* 24.322–467.
11. Hdt. 1.99.1.
12. Hdt. 1.69.1.
13. Hdt. 3.122–123.

14. Chantraine, *Dict. étym.* s.v. πρέσβυς; C. Saerens, *Ant. Class.* 44 (1975) 618–629.

15. Hdt. 3.58.1, 3.

16. Hdt. 5.93.1.

17. Nicolson, *Diplomacy*[2] 60.

18. In general, C. Marek, *Die Proxenie* (Frankfurt, 1984), with summary on 387–391.

19. *Il.* 6.119–236. For guest-friendship, G. Herman in *OCD*[3] 611–613. On the probable Lycian inspiration of the episode, L. Malten, *Hermes* 79 (1944) 1–12.

20. *Il.* 6.145–149. For *geneē*, here probably a synonym of *genos*, see Chapter 1.

21. *Il.* 6.168–169. The word *grapsas*, here translated "inscribing," later means "writing"; "painting" is less likely.

22. *Il.* 6.224–225.

23. See G. F. Bass, *Anat. Stud.* 37 (1987) 217, with reference to the Ulu Burun diptych.

24. F. Parkman, *France and England in North America* (New York: Library of America, 1983) I 228.

25. E.g., *Il.* 2.362–363, with Kirk's commentary.

26. Hellenes: *Il.* 2.684. Panhellenes: *Il.* 2.530.

27. Hes. *Op.* 109–201.

28. M. L. West, *The Hesiodic Catalogue of Women* 57–60.

29. The myths of the Inachids occupy book 2 of Apollodorus' *Library,* on which see Frazer in the Loeb. For the stemma from Hypermestra, daughter of Danaus, to Perseus and Heracles, see J. L. Catterall, *RE* 19 (1937) 979.

30. Hdt. 2.182. On Amasis and the Greeks, H. J. de Meulenaere in *Lexikon der Ägyptologie* I (Wiesbaden, 1975) 182; T. G. H. James, *CAH* 3.2[2] (1991) 725–726, 737.

31. Hdt. 2.91. On Achmim, J. Karig in *Lexikon der Ägyptologie* I 54–55.

32. Cf. West, *Hesiodic Catalogue* 12, 27–28.

33. Hdt. 1.171.6; cf. Str. 14.2.23, 659 C. On this shrine, less celebrated than those of Labraunda and Panamara, A. Adler, *RE* 10 (1919) 1949; A. Laumonier, *Les cultes indigènes en Carie* 41–44.

34. Hdt. 4.145–149, esp. 145.5. On these early myths of Cyrene, Chamoux, *Cyrène sous la monarchie des Battiades* 69–91.
35. Hdt. 5.49–54, esp. 49.1.
36. Hdt. 5.97.2.

3. The Classical Age

1. Hdt. 7.43.
2. Hdt. 7.150; for his expression of doubt, 7.152.3.
3. Aesch. *Pers.* 79.
4. For what follows, see now S. Hornblower, *A Commentary on Thucydides* II 61–80.
5. Thuc. 1.107–108; Diod. Sic. 11.79.5; cf. Hornblower, *Commentary on Thucydides* I 168.
6. *SEG* 38.1476.
7. Thuc. 2.29.3; Schol. Thuc. 127. 15 Hude. Gomme, *A Historical Commentary on Thucydides* II 90, calls this a "characteristically empty comment."
8. G. Hirschfeld, *RE* 1 (1893) 22–23; D. Lazarides in *PECS* 3–4.
9. On the date of Sophocles' *Tereus,* S. Radt, *TGrF* 4 (1977) 436.
10. Thuc. 1.95.1, 3.2.3, 3.86.2, 4.61.2, etc. (Thucydides naturally uses the old Attic forms with *xyn–*). In general, J. H. M. Alty, *JHS* 102 (1982) 1–14; S. Hornblower, *HSCP* 94 (1992) 173–175; O. Curty, *MH* 51 (1994) 193–197.
11. Thuc. 5.104 (Melians), 7.57.1 (Sicilian expedition).
12. Thuc. 4.19.1. See now Hornblower, *Commentary on Thucydides* II 64–65, 175. I do not agree with E. Will, *Rev. Phil.* 69 (1995) 306–307, that φιλίαν πολλήν here refers to friendships between cities other than between the two principals.
13. Thuc. 4.61.2, 4.64.3.
14. Xen. *Anab.* 7.2.31.
15. Xen. *Hell.* 2.4.14, 2.4.17, 2.4.21, 3.2.24, etc.
16. Xen. *Hell.* 6.3, esp. 6.3.6 for Callias' speech. On the historical setting, R. Seager, *CAH* 6^2 (1994) 179–181; for Callias, Davies, *APF* 261–269; K. M. Clinton, *The Sacred Officials of the Eleusinian Mysteries* (Philadelphia, 1974) 49–50.
17. D. Mosley, *PCPhS* 188 (1962) 41–46 (quotation p. 46).
18. For a brief account, J. Roy, *CAH* 6^2 (1994) 187–194.

19. Paus. 10.9.5–6; *FD* 3.1.3–11; cf. C. Habicht, *Pausanias' Guide to Ancient Greece* (Berkeley, 1985) 68.

20. Paus. 10.34.2. On Elatea, A. Philippson, *RE* 5 (1905) 2236–37; S. S. Weinberg in *PECS* 295. For the hero acccompanied by followers, see Chapter 2, and Chapter 6 on Aor; Aeneas is of course another example.

21. Str. 14.1.40, 657 C; Athen. 4.173 E–F = Aristot. fr. 631 Rose.

22. Paus. 8.27.6.

23. In general, F. Chamoux, *Cyrène sous la monarchie des Battiades* chap. 2, "La colonisation légendaire." Inscription: *SEG* 9.3 = Meiggs-Lewis 5; opinions on its authenticity range from virtual acceptance (Meiggs-Lewis) to rejection (Chamoux 108–111; S. Dušanić, *Chiron* 8 [1978] 55–76).

24. C. Habicht, *Hermes* 89 (1961) 11–35, discussing Athens and the Persian Wars.

4. Two Northern Kingdoms

1. For recent examination of the problems, E. Badian in B. Barr-Sharrar and E. N. Borza, eds., *Macedonia and Greece in Late Classical and Early Hellenistic Times* (Washington, DC, 1982) 33–51; on the Macedonian language, N. G. L. Hammond, *Historia* 43 (1994) 131–142; O. Masson, *OCD*³ 905–906.

2. Hdt. 8.138; cf. N. G. L. Hammond, G. T. Griffith, and F. W. Walbank, *A History of Macedonia* II 6–7.

3. Hammond, Griffith, and Walbank, *History of Macedonia* II 30.

4. Hdt. 5.22; Thuc. 2.99.3, 5.80.2.

5. Hdt. 9.45.2.

6. Thuc. 5.80.2.

7. On Archelaus, Gomme, *A Historical Commentary on Thucydides* I 200–201, II 247–248; Hammond, Griffith, and Walbank, *History of Macedonia* II 137–141; for Euripides' *Archelaus,* C. Austin, *Nova Fragmenta Euripidea* (Berlin, 1968) 11–21.

8. Demosth. 9.31.

9. On the historical background, J. R. Ellis, *CAH* 6² (1994) 747–751 (Olynthus), 751–759 (Sacred War).

10. Isocrates does not name the founder (*Philip* 105), but he probably means Caranus, who replaced Perdiccas in this role in the fourth

century; Theopompus, *FGrH* 115 F 393, with Jacoby's commentary; Plut. *Alex.* 2.1, with Hamilton's commentary; Hammond, Griffith, and Walbank, *History of Macedonia* II 11–12.

11. *Philip* 111–112, esp. 111; cf. 115. On this incident, known to Homer but apparently elaborated only much later, J. Boardman, *LIMC* 5.1 (1990) 111–112.

12. *Philip* 32–34, 76–77.

13. *Philip* 15 (Philip has attained what "none of the Greeks" have), 122 (philhellene), 126 (kinship), 32 *(archēgos tou genous)*.

14. *Philip* 106–108.

15. For *phylon* as denoting "the distinctiveness of one entity as opposed to another," G. Nagy, *Greek Mythology and Poetics* (Ithaca, 1990) 290. For Persians as "barbarians," *Philip* 9, 16, 43, etc.

16. Text in E. Bickermann and J. Sykutris, *Speusipps Brief an König Philipp;* M. Isnardi Parente, *Speusippos: Frammenti* (Naples, 1980) 123–127; an extract in Jacoby, *FGrH* 69.

17. *FGrH* 69: clearly not the famous Antipater, general of Philip and Alexander, though he too was a historian (*FGrH* 114). Not in *RE*.

18. Cf. Xen. *Mem.* 1.5.2 (where the speaker is Socrates); Pl. *Alc.* 123 B 4, *Leg.* VI 323 A 4.

19. Speus. *Ep. Phil.* 2; other references in J. Boardman, *LIMC* 4.1 (1988) 805–806 (overlooking this passage).

20. Speus. *Ep. Phil.* 5.

21. G. Le Rider, *Le monnayage d'argent et d'or de Philippe II* (Paris, 1977) 363–368; Hammond, Griffith, and Walbank, *History of Macedonia* II 663–667.

22. Plut. *Alex.* 15.7–9, with Hamilton's commentary; Arr. *Anab.* 1.11.7–12.5, with Bosworth's commentary.

23. Str. 13.1.27, 594 C.; 13.1.26, 593 C.

24. Arr. *Anab.* 1.11.7, with Bosworth's commentary; M. Zahrnt, *Chiron* 26 (1996) 129–147. On Alexander and the heroes, see also P. A. Brunt, *Arrian: History of Alexander and Indica I* (Cambridge, Mass., 1976) 464–466.

25. Diod. Sic. 17.77.1–3 with Welles's note; Plut. *Alex.* 46, with Hamilton's commentary; Arr. *Anab.* 7.13, with Brunt, *Arrian* II (Cambridge, Mass., 1983) 493–495.

26. Arr. *Anab.* 2.5.9, cf. Str. 14.5.16, 675 C; A. R. Bosworth, *A Historical Commentary on Arrian's History of Alexander* I (Oxford, 1980) 198; idem, *Conquest and Empire* (Cambridge, 1988) 58, 254.

27. Str. 11.14.12–14, 530–531 C (*FGrH* 129 F 1); on this passage see L. Robert, *OMS* V 435–437 = *CRAI* 1968. For Armenion, G. Hirschfeld, *RE* 2 (1895) 1187; F. Stählin, *RE* 6 A (1936) 94.

28. Thus P. Högemann, *Alexander der Grosse und Arabien* (Munich, 1985) 124–126, 137–138; Bosworth, *Conquest and Empire* 119, 278.

29. On Nysa, Bosworth, *Conquest and Empire* 121–122; Bosworth, *Historical Commentary* II (Oxford, 1995) 197–199.

30. Priene: *IPriene* 5, with Hiller's commentary. Colophon: *IG* 2/3² 456.

31. For the Molossians, N. G. L. Hammond, *Epirus* (Oxford, 1967) 525–540; idem, *CAH* 6² (1994) 430–443. For Pyrrhus/Neoptolemus, O. Touchefeu-Meynier, *LIMC* 6.1 (1992) 773–775. Pindar: *Nem.* 4.51, 7.38–40, *Paean* 6.100–120; Euripides: *Androm. 1243–52; Hellanicus: Dion. Hal. 1.72.2* = *FGrH* 4 F 84. For Trojan place-names in Epirus, L. Robert, *Hellenica* 1 (1940) 95–105.

32. For Tharyps, B. Lenk, *RE* 16 (1933) 20; Gomme, *Historical Commentary on Thucydides* II 214–215; Hammond, *Epirus* 507–508. Tharyps was an Athenian citizen: *IG* 2/3² 226, 2 (Tod, *GHI* II 173).

33. On Epirus in this period, Lenk, *RE* 16 (1933) 21–24; Tod, *GHI* II pp. 216–217; P. Lévêque, *Pyrrhos* 83–89, with stemma of the kings, 84; D. Kienast, *RE* 24 (1963) 112–115.

34. O. Walter, *JÖAI* 32 (1940) 1–24.

35. On Alexander, the principal ancient source is Livy 8.3.6–7, 8.17.9–10 (treaty), 8.24.1–18. See also *CAH* 6² (1994) 391–392 (N. Purcell), 440–441 (N. G. L. Hammond).

36. Lévêque, *Pyrrhos,* remains fundamental; see also Kienast, *RE* 24 (1963) 108–165; P. R. Franke, *CAH* 7.2² (1989) 456–485. On Proxenus, Lévêque 28–32; the fragments are in *FGrH* 703. For the first Lanassa, M. Schmidt, *RE* 12 (1923) 617 no. 1; for the second, F. Stähelin, ibid. 617–618 no. 2.

37. Paus 1.12.2. Coins: B. V. Head, *A Guide to the Principal Coins of*

the Greeks (London, 1932) 67, no. C 19, with plate 37; Lévêque, *Pyrrhos* plate VI nos. 8, 9; Franke, *CAH* 7.2² (1989) 465.

38. Cic. *Div.* 2.116 = Ennius *Ann.* VI fr. iv Skutsch. In favor of authenticity, Lévêque, *Pyrrhos* 273–274; against, Skutsch pp. 333–334. For Pyrrhus and Dodona, Hammond, *Epirus* 582–583; Y. Béquignon in *PECS* 279–280.

39. Dorieus: Hdt. 5.43. Pyrrhus at Eryx: Diod. Sic. 22.10.3; Plut. *Pyrrh.* 22.7–12 (from whom comes the quotation in the text). Cf. Lévêque, *Pyrrhos* 479–480; Kienast, *RE* 24 (1963) 150. On Eryx in the First Punic War, see Chapter 7.

40. See now the edition of M. Fusillo, A. Hurst, and G. Paduano (Milan, 1991); good discussion also by A. W. Bulloch, *CHCL* 1 (1985) 548–549; and A. Bernardi, *Enc. Virg.* 3 (1987) 215–216. Note also P. M. Fraser, *OCD*³ 895–897, who thinks the poem written by a pseudo-Lycophron in the early second century, incorporating "some of the literary substance" of the real Lycophron.

41. Lyc. *Alex.* 1228–30, 1446–50. The latter, very obscure lines are the chief argument for dating the poem, in whole or in part, to the second century, the reference being to T. Flamininus. I have tried to retain the ambiguity of *diallagai,* which might mean "exchange" and not only "reconciliation."

5. Cities, Leagues, and Kings

1. For an excellent general history, F. W. Walbank, *The Hellenistic World*² (Cambridge, Mass., 1993); on the political history, E. Will, *Histoire politique du monde hellénistique*²; idem, II 13: "Le moment où les destinés du monde hellénistique changent de cours se place le jour de l'été de 200 où le Peuple romain vota la guerre." Similarly, C. Habicht, *Athens from Alexander to Antony* 197–198.

2. *IMagnesia* 61 line 36 = *OGIS* 233; Curty, *Parentés* 46a; K. J. Rigsby, *Asylia: Territorial Inviolability in the Hellenistic World* 111.

3. On the circumstances, P. S. Derow, *ZPE* 88 (1991) 261–270 = *SEG* 41.545; cf. Curty, *Parentés* 37.

4. *IMagnesia* 16 = *Syll.*³ 557.

5. D. Musti, *Ann. Sc. Norm. Pisa* 32 (1963) 225–239.

6. Istria: Robert, *OMS* I 99–101 = *BCH* 1928; Curty, *Parentés* 54.

7. Theocr. 18.13–33.

8. Argos and Rhodes: L. Moretti, *Iscrizioni storiche ellenistiche* I 40 = Curty, *Parentés* 4.

9. Pindar *Ol.* 7.20–31, Thuc. 7.57.6.

10. L. Robert, *Documents d'Asie Mineure* 173–186, proving that the Heraclea in question is the city of northwestern Caria; Curty, *Parentés* 15.

11. For the myth, Robert, *Documents* 185–186; H. Gabelmann, *LIMC* 3.1 (1986) 726–728.

12. For the Argive Iasus, G. Weicker, *RE* 9 (1914) 784, Iasos 4; for the founder of Iasus, R. Vollkommer, *LIMC* 5.1 (1990) 638.

13. M. Holleaux, *Etudes d'épigraphie et d'histoire grecques* IV (Paris, 1952) 148–162; Curty, *Parentés* 63; A. Meadows, *Chiron* 26 (1996) 251–265, esp. 260–261.

14. Livy 37.17: "urbem cognatam, suas necessitudines memorando"; cf. Holleaux, *Etudes* IV 315, 326–327.

15. *Milet* 1.3: *Delphinion* 37 = Curty, *Parentés* 56.

16. Miletus: R. Vollkommer, *LIMC* 6.1 (1992) 568–569; Nicander, fr. 46 Schneider.

17. On this subject, Walbank, *HCP* III 335–336; L. Robert, *OMS* V 137–154; P. Gauthier, *Nouvelles inscriptions de Sardes* 2 (Geneva, 1989) 121–124; C. Crowther, *Journal of Ancient Civilizations* 8 (1993) 40–77 *(non vidi)*, analyzed by P. Gauthier, *Bull. épigr.* 1995 493.

18. In Curty, *Parentés,* 9, 11, 18, 19, 26, etc. I am very grateful to C. Crowther for discussion on this point.

19. *IG* 9^2 1.3, 609 = Meiggs-Lewis 13.

20. In general, E. Schlesinger, *Die griechische Asylie* (Diss. Giessen, 1933); K. J. Rigsby, *Asylia* 1–29. On the importance of the right of seizure in these appeals, B. Bravo, *Ann. Sc. Norm. Pisa* 10 (1980) 675–987; P. Gauthier, *Revue historique des droits français et étranger* 60 (1982) 553–576.

21. Curty, *Parentés* 27, with his discussion; Rigsby, *Asylia* 154–163.

22. The earliest datable reply is from Ptolemy II Philadelphus: Welles, *RC* 21; R. Herzog and G. Klaffenbach, *Asylieurkunden*

aus Kos (Berlin, 1952) 1; Rigsby, *Asylia* 13, proposing Ptolemy III. On the chronology of these appeals, Herzog and Klaffenbach 27–28; Curty, *Parentés* 49–52; Rigsby 106–111.

23. Herzog and Klaffenbach, *Asylieurkunden* 3 = Curty, *Parentés* 24e; Rigsby, *Asylia* 12, with the discussion of J. and L. Robert, *Bull. épigr.* 1953 156–157, 1966 305, 1976 522. Athens and Spartocus: *IG* 2/3² 653 = *Syll.*³ 370; cf. Habicht, *Athens* 135–136.

24. Herzog and Klaffenbach, *Asylieurkunden* 12 (Camarina), 13 (Gela) = Curty, *Parentés* 24a, 24b; Rigsby, *Asylia* 48, 49. In general, H. D. Westlake, *CAH* 6² (1994) 716–718.

25. Herzog and Klaffenbach, *Asylieurkunden* 6 (Cassandreia, Amphipolis, Philippi), 7 (Pella) = Rigsby, *Asylia* 23, 25–27.

26. Classic discussion by M. Holleaux, *CAH* 8 (1930) 132–166 = *Etudes d'histoire* V 313–351; cf. also Will, *Histoire politique*² 101–149; Habicht, *Athens* 190, 194–195.

27. On the prize system of Greek contests and the difference between those offering money *(thematitai)* and crowns *(stephanitai)*, L. Robert, *OMS* VI 710–719. Chronology: J. Ebert, *Philologus* 126 (1982) 198–216, cf. J. and L. Robert, *Bull. épigr.* 1983 342; Rigsby, *Asylia* 179–181. Mythic history: *IMagnesia* 17. Cretan decree: *IMagnesia* 20. Cf. also A. Chaniotis, *Historie und Historiker in den griechischen Inschriften* 34–40.

28. Thessaly: *IMagnesia* 26 (using the synonym *homogeneia*) = Rigsby, *Asylia* 75, 33 (Curty, *Parentés* 46e, Rigsby, *Asylia* 83). Lesbian city: *IMagnesia* 52 (Curty 46g; Rigsby 101). Same: *IMagnesia* 35 = Curty 46c.

29. On this phenomenon, L. Robert, *A travers l'Asie Mineure* 418; C. P. Jones, *Phoenix* 47 (1993) 303–304.

30. *IMagnesia* 61 = *OGIS* 233; Curty, *Parentés* 46a; Rigsby, *Asylia* 111. Cf. the answer from Antioch on the Maeander: *IMagnesia* 79, 80 = Curty 46b; Rigsby 125.

31. The chief evidence is a famous inscription published by P. Herrmann, *Anadolu* 9 (1965) 29–160 = *SEG* 41.1003, where the question of the dating is summarized; cf. Rigsby, *Asylia* 281–285.

32. The vulnerability of Teos is well illustrated by a recently published inscription, apparently of the later second century: S.

Şahin, *Epigraphica Anatolica* 23 (1994) 1–36, with the discussion of P. Gauthier, *Bull. épigr.* 1996 353.

33. Delphi: *OGIS* 234 = Curty, *Parentés* 13; Rigsby, *Asylia* 163. Athens: R. Pounder, *Hesperia* 47 (1978) 49–57 = *SEG* 28.75; Rigsby 162. Chronology: Rigsby 326–330.

34. On this league, the chief ancient text is Str. 14.2.25, 660 C; J. and L. Robert, *Fouilles d'Amyzon en Carie* 223–225; J. Bousquet, *REG* 101 (1988) 36–37.

35. Bousquet, *REG* 101 (1988) 12–53; *SEG* 38.1476, 39.475; Curty, *Parentés* 75; see also Chapter 3 and Appendix 1.

36. *SEG* 38.1476 14–33.

37. *Milet* 1.3: *Delphinion* 155 = Curty, *Parentés* 58, with bibliography.

38. *CIG* 2878; see G. W. Bowersock, *Bonner Historia-Augusta Colloquium 1982–1983* 81.

39. L. Robert, *Etudes anatoliennes* (Paris, 1937) 552–555.

40. L. Robert, *OMS* VII 283–295; B. C. McGing, *The Foreign Policy of Mithridates VI Eupator* 89–95, 107–108; Habicht, *Athens* 297–304. For Athena as a divine helper of Perseus, Pherec. *FGrH* 3 F 11; Pind. *Pyth.* 10.45; Apollod. *Bibl.* 2.4.2–3; L. Jones Roccos, *LIMC* 7.1 (1994) 341–342.

6. Lycians and Jews

1. Hom. *Il.* 6.152.

2. M. J. Mellink, *AJA* 74 (1970) 251–253, with plate 61, fig. 30; Mellink, *Rev. Arch.* 1976 28–29. For the myth, Hes. *Theog.* 281.

3. The tradition is first mentioned by the Corinthian Eumelos in the eighth century; A. Bernabé, *Poet. Ep. Gr.* Eumelos 1, 4; cf. G. S. Kirk, *The Iliad: A Commentary* 2 (Cambridge, 1990) 177.

4. Hdt. 1.173.3.

5. Bernabé, *Poet. Ep. Gr.* Panyassis 23; see Appendix 2.

6. Aeneas and Pandarus: Hom. *Il.* 2.819–827, 5.166–317. Later honors: Str. 14.3.5, 665 C.

7. *Il.* 20.307–308, cf. *Hymn. Hom. Ven.* 196–197; M. W. Edwards, *The Iliad: A Commentary* 5 (Cambridge, 1991) 299–301.

8. Dion. Hal. *Ant. Rom.* 1.48.3 = *FGrH* 799 F 3.

9. C. P. Jones in *Studies for Dante* 19–23.

10. For the inscription of the Cytenian ambassadors, Chapter 5; on the Chrysaorian league, Appendix 1.

11. *OGIS* 746; *TAM* 2.1, 266; J. and L. Robert, *Fouilles d'Amyzon en Carie* 161.

12. P. Gauthier and J.-L. Ferrary, *Journal des savants* 1981 327–345, discussing *Illion* 45; C. P. Jones, *GRBS* 34 (1993) 73–92, discussing *Illion* 32 = *OGIS* 219.

13. J. and L. Robert, *Fouilles d'Amyzon* 154–163; Curty, *Parentés* 76.

14. Plb. 22.5. So understood, for example, by E. S. Shuckburgh in his translation, and by J. and L. Robert, *Fouilles d'Amyzon* 162, whereas Paton in the Loeb translates "for the sake of the kinship between Ilion and Rome"; followed by Walbank, *HCP* III 182–183. S. Elwyn, *TAPA* 123 (1993) 275–276, understands the kinship as involving all three parties, Ilians, Lycians, and Romans.

15. Plb. 30.6.12; Walbank, *HCP* III 427.

16. Best text in A. Degrassi, *Bull. Comm. Arch. Roma* 74 (1951–52) 19–47; convenient summary in Degrassi, *ILLRP*[2] I 114–123; on the date, R. Mellor, *Chiron* 8 (1978) 319–330. See further S. Elwyn, *TAPA* 123 (1993) 275–276; C. P. Jones in *Studies for Dante*.

17. Dessau, *ILS* 31, 32 = Degrassi, *ILLRP*[2] I 174, 175.

18. Verg. *Aen.* 1.113–117.

19. Strabo: 14.3.2–3, 664–665 C; cf. R. Syme, *Roman Papers* IV (Oxford, 1988) 121. Troubles under Claudius: Suet. *Claud.* 25.3, Cass. Dio 60.17.3. Diplomacy, Tlos and Xanthus: *TAM* II 555 = Curty, *Parentés* 78; Sidyma and Tlos: *TAM* II 174 = Curty 79. Lyciarch: Philostratus *Vit. Soph.* 2.26, 112 Kayser.

20. D. I. Pallas, S. Charitonidis, and J. Venencie, *BCH* 83 (1959) 496–508 = *SEG* 18.143, with the discussion of L. Robert, *OMS* II 840–848.

21. For excellent treatments of these events, W. Otto, *RE* 7 (1912) 2491–2501; E. Will, *Histoire politique du monde hellénistique*[2] II 326–344; E. Schürer, *The History of the Jewish People in the Age of Jesus Christ*[2] I 125–188; C. Habicht, *CAH* 8[2] (1989) 346–350, 362–370.

22. For recent discussions, O. Curty, *Historia* 41 (1992) 246–248; E. Gruen in *Transitions to Empire* 254–270.

23. Jos. *Ap.* 1.176–182; M. Stern, *Greek and Roman Authors on Jews and Judaism* I 47–52.

24. F. Jacoby, *RE* 7 (1912) 2750–69; A. Momigliano, *Alien Wisdom* 83–84; W. Spoerri, *RAC* 14 (1988) 275–310; fragments in *FGrH* 264, Stern, *Greek and Roman Authors* I 20–44.

25. Diod. Sic. 40.3; *FGrH* 264 F 6.2; Stern, *Greek and Roman Authors* I 26–35.

26. In general, O. Waser, *RE* 4 (1901) 2094–98; E. Keuls, *LIMC* 3.1 (1986) 341–343.

27. Diod. Sic. 40.3.6–7; *FGrH* 264 F 6.

28. See Chapter 3 on Nymphodorus of Abdera. Note also Abdera's use of its historical mother city, Teos in Ionia, to plead on its behalf with the Roman senate: *Syll.*³ 656, with the discussions of L. Robert, *OMS* I 320–326 = *BCH* 1935; and C. Marek, *Tyche* 12 (1997) 169–177.

29. Courtier of Ptolemy: Jos. *Ap.* 1.183; cf. Diod. Sic. 1.46.8 = *FGrH* 264 T 7, 4. Embassy to Sparta: Plut. *Lyc.* 20.3 (T 5). Cf. Fraser, *Ptol. Alex.* 504–505.

30. Hom. *Od.* 4.81–85; 1 Kings 6–9; Menander in Tatianus, *Ad Gr.* 37 = *FGrH* 783 F 2. In general, Stern, *Greek and Roman Authors* I 119–122.

31. Again, the subject is vast and controversial. Note esp. E. Bickermann, *RE* 14 (1928) 779–797; Schürer, *History*² III.1 180–185 (1 Macc.), 531–537 (2 Macc.), 545–546 (Josephus).

32. 1 Macc. 12:19–23; Jos. *AJ* 12.226–227. For Josephus' methods of stylistic adaptation, A. Pelletier, *Flavius Josèphe, adaptateur de la Lettre d'Aristée* (Paris, 1962) 251–276.

33. For Areus, see now Cartledge in P. Cartledge and A. J. Spawforth, *Hellenistic and Roman Sparta* (London, 1989) 28–37. On the dating of the high priests beginning with Jaddua, Schürer, *History*² I 139 n. 3.

34. On this problem, see most recently Gruen in *Transitions to Empire* 256–257. On the ambiguous term "forgery," T. D. Barnes, *Historia* 44 (1995) 497–500.

35. Gen. 22:17–18.

36. Jos. *AJ* 1.241 = *FGrH* 727. On Cleodemus, Schürer, *History*² III.1 526–528.

37. This too has accumulated a huge literature: text by A. Pelletier, *Sources chrétiennes* 89 (1962); surveys by O. Murray, *RAC* Suppl. 1 (1986) 573–587; Schürer, *History*[2] III.1 677–688.

38. *Ep. Arist.* 40.

39. *IMagnesia* 20, on which see Chapter 5; adduced by E. Bickermann, *RE* 14 (1928) 786.

40. Correctly observed by Momigliano, *Alien Wisdom* 113: "The family link between the Jews and the Spartans was not invented by the Hasmoneans . . . but it fell to the lot of the Hasmoneans to exploit this legend for political respectability."

41. 2 Macc. 5.9.

42. L. Robert, *Noms indigènes dans l'Asie-Mineure gréco-romaine* (Paris, 1963) 227–228 (Tlepolemus), index s.v. "Héros et anthroponymes."

43. 1 Macc. 12.5–23 (letter of Jonathan), 14.17–23 (Spartan reply).

44. Jos. *AJ* 13.167. πεπιστεῦσθαι, which should here mean "was confirmed," may be an error for πεπιστῶσθαι. For *apodeixis* as "public presentation," G. Nagy, *Pindar's Homer* (Baltimore, 1990) 220–224.

45. *SEG* 38.1478.30–32; see Chapter 5.

46. *SEG* 12.379.19–23 = Curty, *Parentés* no. 24a; Rigsby, *Asylia* 48. For other parallels, and coming to the same conclusion, L. V. Semenchenko, *Vestnik drevnei istorii* 1993, fasc. 2, 105–111.

47. 1 Macc. 14:20–23; thus Momigliano, *Alien Wisdom* 113–114.

48. *IMagnesia* 33 = Curty, *Parentés* 46e; Rigsby, *Asylia* 83.

49. 1 Macc. 8; cf. Momigliano, *Alien Wisdom* 114.

50. In general, F. Bölte, *RE* 6 A (1929) 1440–45; Will, *Histoire politique*[2] II 390–400; Cartledge, *Hellenistic and Roman Sparta* 77–90. Sparta after 146: Str. 8.5.5, 365 C; Paus. 7.16.10.

51. *Syll.*[3] 591 = Curty, *Parentés* 39.

52. Jos. *AJ* 14.247–255; cf. Schürer, *History*[2] I 204–205; T. Rajak, *GRBS* 22 (1981) 78–79. The *prytanis* Cratippus mentioned in this text probably belonged to a distinguished Pergamene family, cf. C. Habicht, *IPergamon (Asklepieion)* 164–165.

53. *IPergamon* 156 = Curty, *Parentés* 41; cf. Robert, *OMS* I 453–454 (*REG* 1927), VI 462–464 (*Rev. Phil.* 1984). The inner face of the the Great Altar of Pergamum has famous reliefs showing this legend: T. S. Scheer, *Mythische Vorväter* 110–152; R. Dreyfus and E.

Schraudolph, eds., *Pergamon: The Telephos Frieze from the Great Altar,* 2 vols. (San Francisco, 1996–1997).

54. T. Bryce, *The Lycians in Literary and Epigraphic Sources* (Copenhagen, 1986) 54; the last surviving inscription is from about 330.

7. The Roman Republic

1. Shirley J. Schwarz, *LIMC* 5.1 (1990) 196–198.

2. On Stesichorus' origin, D. A. Campbell, *Greek Lyric* (Loeb) 3 (1991) 2–3; for the fragments of his *Geryoneis,* 65–89.

3. Verg. *Aen.* 8.184–275. Stesichorus' *Geryoneis* referred to Pallantion, the mythical home of Evander: Paus. 8.3.2 = S 85 Campbell.

4. Shown by a painted inscription from Tauromenium (Taormina), *SEG* 26.1123.

5. On the Dioscuri, A. Hermary, *LIMC* 3.1 (1986) 567–568. Lake Regillus: Livy 2.20.12, with Ogilvie's commentary; Dion. Hal. *Ant. Rom.* 6.13. Inscription of Lanuvium: Degrassi, *ILLRP*[2] II 1271a.

6. Resentment: Hom. *Il.* 13.460–461, 20.179–183. Prophecy of Poseidon: 20.307–308. In general, F. Canciani, *LIMC* 1.1 (1981) 381; S. J. Harrison, *OCD*[3] 22–23.

7. Dion. Hal. *Ant. Rom.* 1.72.2 = *FGrH* 4 F 84, with Jacoby's apparatus (one manuscript reads "*after* Odysseus"). In general, T. P. Wiseman, *Remus: A Roman Myth* (Cambridge, 1995) 50–52.

8. Plut. *Ant.* 4.1–2.

9. Str. 5.4.12, 250 C: the verb translated "win over" (ἐξοικειούμενοι) might mean "assimilate." On this incident see now E. Dench, *From Barbarians to New Men* 53–54.

10. Str. 5.3.5, 232 C (Strabo's simple "Demetrius" must indicate Poliorcetes).

11. Thus G. de Sanctis, *Storia dei Romani* 2 (1907) 427: "flosculi retorici di Timeo." A. Alföldi, however, considers the tradition "wohl glaubhaft": *Die Trojanischen Urahnen der Römer* (Basel, 1957) 28.

12. Plb. 9.2.1; cf. 34.1.3–6. Cf. 5.76.11, where the Selgians of Pisidia are praised for fighting in a manner worthy of their kinship with the Spartans.

13. Plb. 1.13.1, with Walbank, *HCP* I 64.

14. Thuc. 6.2.3, with A. W. Gomme, A. Andrewes, and K. J. Dover, *A Historical Commentary on Thucydides* IV 211–212.

15. For the city, C. Hülsen, *RE* 6 (1907) 602–604; V. Tusa in *PECS* 317–318. Hero: K. Tümpel, *RE* 6 (1907) 604–606; H. A. Cahn and I. Krauskopf, *LIMC* 4.1 (1988) 22.

16. On the city, K. Ziegler, *RE* 2 A (1921) 1055–69; V. Tusa in *PECS* 817–818. Foundation-legends: J. Toepffer, *RE* 1 (1893) 951–952.

17. Defection of Segesta to Romans: Zonar. 8.9.12 = Dio Cass. I 150 Boissevain; cf. Cic. *II Verr.* 4.72, 5.83. Siege: Plb. 1.24.2, with Walbank, *HCP* I 79–80.

18. Plb. 1.55.6–10 (sanctuary and capture by Romans), 1.58.2–9 (struggle).

19. Cic. *II Verr.* 4.33.72; Tac. *Ann.* 4.43.4.

20. Diod. Sic. 4.83. On this passage, and for the correct interpretation of χρυσοφορεῖν, D. Kienast, *Hermes* 93 (1965) 485–486, following A. Wilhelm.

21. In general, R. Schilling, *La religion romaine de Vénus* 234–266, esp. 235 on the coin of M. Considius Nonianus, plate XXVII 1.

22. Just. *Epit.* 28.1.5–6 (plea); Plb. 2.12.7 (involvement); thus Walbank, *HCP* I 166; E. S. Gruen, *The Hellenistic World and the Coming of Rome* 64.

23. Suet. *Claud.* 25.3; cf. J.-L. Ferrary, *Philhellénisme et impérialisme* 225 n. 11; and (for a less sceptical view) Gruen, *Hellenistic World* 64–65.

24. Isthmia: Zonar. 8.19.7 = Dio Cass. I 182 Boissevain; cf. Walbank, *HCP* I 167.

25. Plb. 2.12.7–8; cf. 2.2.1.

26. Betrayal: e.g., Menecrates of Lycia: Dion. Hal. *Ant. Rom.* 1.48.3 = *FGrH* 769 F 3, with the discussion of D. Asheri, *Fra Ellenismo e Iranismo* 144–153. Odysseus: Hellan. *FGrH* 4 F 84.

27. Plb. 5.104.5, translated as "part and parcel of your own dominions" by W. Paton in the Loeb. For *oikeios* and *prosēkōn* in the imperial period, see Chapter 8.

28. Plb. 9.28–31. On the historical background, Walbank, *HCP* II 162–163.

29. Plb. 9.32–39, esp. 37.6–7, 10, cf. 5.104.10 (Agelaus). Themistocles: Hdt. 8.109.2.

30. Plb. 9.42.5–8; Walbank, *HCP* II 186; cf. III 190. The Aeginetan decree *IG* 2/3² 885, referring to "the kinship between Heracles and Aeacus," appears to provide a mythological justification for the purchase; cf. T. S. Scheer, *Mythische Vorväter* 127–128.

31. Most of the texts in Jacoby, *FGrH* 809; cf. D. Timpe in *ANRW* 1.2 (1972) 928–969; A. Alföldy, *Early Rome and the Latins* (Ann Arbor, 1965) 123–175; B. W. Frier, *Libri Annales Pontificum Maximorum* (Rome, 1979) 227–253; Gruen, *Hellenistic World* 253–255.

32. Heracles in Italy: *SEG* 26.1123; *Bull. ép.* 1976 820. Site of Rome: Dion. Hal. *Ant. Rom.* 1.31.3, with Walbank, *HCP* I 664–665.

33. This is revealed by the inscription of Tauromenium (*SEG* 26.1123); see C. P. Jones, *HSCP* 97 (1995) 235 n. 12, suggesting "Latinos" instead of "Lanoios."

34. *Serv. Dan.* on Verg. *Aen.* 5.73 = *FGrH* 809 F 28.

35. Plut. *Flam.* 12.11–12 = D. L. Page, *Further Greek Epigrams* (Cambridge, 1981) 477–478.

36. *SEG* 30.1073; *Bull. ép.* 1980 353, 1981 364, 1984 306.

37. Caes. *BG* 1.33.2: "fratres consanguineosque saepenumero a senatu appellatos"; Tac. *Ann.* 11.25.1. In general, S. Elwyn, *TAPA* 123 (1993) 278–279.

38. *Paneg. Lat.* 8(5).3.1; cf. the Conclusion in this volume. There is no good reason to suppose Lucan to be wrong in saying that the enemies of the Aedui, the Arverni, falsely claimed descent from Troy (*Phars.* 1.427–428); this may be a counterclaim to that of a rival tribe.

39. Claudius: Tac. *Ann.* 11.25.1. On the interpretation of this passage, F. Millar, *The Emperor in the Roman World* (London, 1977) 293.

40. G. Manganaro, *Rendic. Accad. Arch. Napoli* 1963 (1964) 23–44; *Ann. épigr.* 1966 165; *Bull. ép.* 1965 499 (essential changes to the text); cf. S. Elwyn, *TAPA* 123 (1993) 276–278. Centuripae as Latin colony: Pliny, *NH* 3.91.

41. M. Holleaux, *CAH* 8 (1930) 179: "The Lampsacenes conveniently discovered that, as inhabitants of Troas, they had blood-ties with Rome . . . Despite these elements of comedy, the action of Lampsacus and Smyrna was a momentous new departure."

8. Two Cities

1. For the compact of 60 B.C., R. Syme, *The Roman Revolution* (Oxford, 1939) 8; for the popular vote of 200, E. Will, *Histoire politique du monde hellénistique²* I 13.

2. On this league see above all D. Magie, *Roman Rule in Asia Minor* II (Princeton, 1950) 869–871; L. Robert, *Monnaies antiques en Troade* 18–46.

3. Livy 29.12.14 (inclusion of Ilium), 29.11.1 (lack of allies in Asia). Against Livy on this point, J.-L. Ferrary, *Philhellénisme et impérialisme* 25 n. 81; C. Habicht, *Athens from Alexander to Antony* 195–196.

4. Appeal of Lampsacus: *ILampsakos* 4 = *Syll.³* 591; cf. Magie, *Roman Rule* 105–106, 947 n. 51; Walbank, *HCP* II 614, 620–21; Ferrary, *Philhellénisme* 133–141; E. S. Gruen, *The Hellenistic World and the Coming of Rome* index s.v. *Syll.³* 591; J. Linderski in E. Frézouls and A. Jacquemin, eds., *Les relations internationales* (Paris, 1995) 472–474. On Massilia, F. Salviat in *PECS* 557–558; cf. L. Robert, *OMS* VII 141–157, on Massilia's cultural connections and links with Ionia. On Elea, L. Richardson Jr. in *PECS* 295–296; K. Lomas in *OCD³* 516.

5. Scipio received by the Ilians: Livy 37.37.3. Commissioners: Livy 38.39.10. Aeneas: Hom. *Il.* 2.819, Dion. Hal. *Ant. Rom.* 1.46.1 = Hellanicus, *FGrH* 4 F 31. Cf. T. S. MacKay in *PECS* 258, s.v. "Dardanos."

6. Str. 13.1.27, 594 C.

7. Robert, *Monnaies antiques en Troade,* esp. 39–41.

8. The date of this rebuilding has been placed by some as late as the reign of Augustus, who certainly repaired the temple. On this disputed question, B. Schmidt-Dounas, *Ist. Mitt.* 41 (1991) 363–369; C. Brian Rose, *Studia Troica* 2 (1992) 45–46.

9. S. Weinstock, *Divus Julius* (Oxford, 1971) 17–18.

10. Exemption: *Illion* 71 = *OGIS* 440; *ILS* 8770; *IGRom* IV 194.

11. *Illion* 10 = *OGIS* 444; cf. Robert, *Monnaies antiques en Troade* 15–17.

12. App. *Mithr.* 53.211, more candid than Str. 13.1.27, 594 C. Cf.

B. C. McGing, *The Foreign Policy of Mithridates VI Eupator* 111–112.

13. Fimbria: App. *Mithr.* 53.213. Sulla: Str. 13.1.27, 594 C.

14. Str. 13.1.27, 594–595 C.

15. Temple of Athena: *Illion* 84; cf. C. Brian Rose, *Studia Troica* 2 (1992) 45. Concert hall and council chamber: Rose, *Studia Troica* 4 (1994) 89–90. A superb head of Augustus was recently found in the ruins of the concert hall; J. N. Wilford, "Third Defense Line Found at Troy," *New York Times,* 16 September 1997.

16. *IGRom* IV 200, 204, 205, 207, 209 = *Illion* 82 (Augustus), 86 (Agrippa), 87 (Gaius Caesar), 89 (Tiberius), 91 (family group of Claudius, in which only Nero is "cousin"). "Benefactor," "guest": *IGRom* IV 201, 203 = *Illion* 81, 83.

17. Nic. Dam., *FGrH* 90 F 134.

18. Tac. *Ann.* 12.58.1.

19. On this, J. M. Cook, *The Troad* (Oxford, 1973) 198–204; C. P. Jones, *CP* 80 (1985) 42 n. 12; E. Schwertheim et al., eds., *Die Troas: Neue Forschungen zu Neandria und Alexandria Troas,* 2 vols. (Bonn, 1994–1996).

20. For an overview of the site and its history, K. T. Erim, *Aphrodisias: City of Venus Aphrodite* (London, 1986); on the current excavations, R. R. R. Smith and C. Ratté, *AJA* 101 (1997) 1–22. Most of the inscriptions discussed in the text are in J. M. Reynolds, *Aphrodisias and Rome.* Aphrodite ancestor of the Romans in general: Reynolds, *Aphrodisias* 55 = *SEG* 30.1254; Aphrodite ancestor of the emperors: Reynolds, *Aphrodisias* 54 (*SEG* 30.1253); *SEG* 36.968.

21. C. Habicht, *MDAI(A)* 72 (1957) 245–249; *Bull. ép.* 1960 318; L. Robert in *Etudes déliennes* (1973) 446–451; M. Errington, *Chiron* 17 (1987) 103–105.

22. Reynolds, *Aphrodisias* 1; *SEG* 32.1097; Reynolds, *REA* 87 (1985) 213–218.

23. App. *Bell. Civ.* 1.453–455. Ax: J. Schaefer, *De Iove apud Cares culto* 367–369; for illustrations, *BMC Greek Coins: Caria* 25. For gold as the metal of the gods, H.-J. Horn, *RAC* 11 (1981) 898–900, esp. 898 on "golden" Aphrodite.

24. Reynolds, *Aphrodisias* 5–6 and nos. 8, 41, and 35 *(asylia)*, 12, 13

(Eros), 32 (statue of Victory). On the *asylia* of Aphrodisias, K. J. Rigsby, *Asylia* 428–432.

25. Monument of Zoilus, R. R. R. Smith, *Aphrodisias* I: *The Monument of C. Julius Zoilus* (Mainz, 1993), esp. 53–54 on Minos.

26. R. R. R. Smith, *JRS* 77 (1987) 89–98.

27. J. M. Reynolds, *Studi clasice* 24 (1986) 111–113; *SEG* 36.968, 969.

28. J. M. Reynolds, *PCPS* 206 (1980) 80–82; *SEG* 30.1247, 1249–52.

29. Reynolds, *PCPS* 206 (1980) 74–76; *SEG* 30.1254; Reynolds, *Aphrodisias* 55.

30. On the date at which the collection of documents was begun, G. W. Bowersock, *Gnomon* 56 (1984) 50–51.

31. A letter of Hadrian from 119 refers back to such a letter, which is not inscribed: Reynolds, *Aphrodisias* 15.

32. Ibid. 17.

33. For cities, bibliography in L. Robert, *Documents d'Asie Mineure* 68 n. 106; for persons: idem, *A travers l'Asie Mineure* 246. See also J. H. M. Strubbe, *Ancient Society* 15–17 (1984–1986) 253–254.

34. Justin. *Nov.* 78.5.

35. Reynolds, *Aphrodisias* 18.

36. Above, Chapter 7. When used of blood relationships, the meaning is often qualified by some phrase such as κατὰ γένος, e.g., Plut. *Thes.* 19.9.

37. Reynolds, *Aphrodisias* 20.

38. Ibid. 25.

39. On such titles, Robert, *Documents d'Asie Mineure* 88; P. Herrmann, *Chiron* 23 (1993) 235 n. 6.

40. Tac. *Ann.* 3.62.2. On the problems of this passage, Reynolds, *Aphrodisias* 79–80, Rigsby, *Asylia* 429, 585.

41. *CIG* 3612 = *Illion* 102 (between 4 and 23).

9. The Roman Empire

1. Strabo 14.3.3, 665 C, discussing the Lycian League; cf. Plut. *Praec. ger. reip.* 805 A.

2. Tac. *Ann.* 3.60.1: "imago antiquitatis."

3. For families claiming descent from heroes, see, e.g., *IG*² 4.1, 86, and later in this chapter on Marcus of Byzantium. In general, J. H. M. Strubbe, *Ancient Society* 15–17 (1984–1986) 253–304.

4. On this development, L. Robert, *OMS* VI 452–455.

5. *Illion* 102.

6. Above, Chapter 8.

7. For the argument that Tacitus had served in both these provinces as proconsular legate, G. W. Bowersock in T. J. Luce and A. J. Woodman, eds., *Tacitus and the Tacitean Tradition* (Princeton, 1993) 3–10 = *Studies on the Eastern Roman Empire* (Goldbach bei Aschaffenberg, 1994) 353–361.

8. Strabo 14.1.23, 641 C; K. J. Rigsby, *Asylia* 389–390.

9. Tac. *Ann.* 3.61; on these transactions, see esp. D. Magie, *Roman Rule in Asia Minor* I (Princeton, 1950) 503–505; Rigsby, *Asylia* 2–3, 29, and, on Ephesus, 386–387. On the site of Ortygia, J. Keil, *JÖAI* 21–22 (1922–1924) 113–119; Tacitus' account does not clearly distinguish the two sites. Stratonicea in Caria also claimed immunity for two sanctuaries, of Zeus at Panamara and of Hecate at Lagina; Tac. *Ann.* 3.62.2.

10. Cf. Tacitus' observation, "Decrees of the senate were framed full of reverence towards the cities . . . so that they should not fall into competition under the mask of religion"; *Ann.* 3.63.4.

11. Tac. *Ann.* 4.15, 4.55–56. Cf. Magie, *Roman Rule* 501–502.

12. On the Etruscan league in the imperial period, B. Liou, *Praetores Etruriae XV populorum* (Brussels, 1969), esp. 95–96 on the date of the reconstitution.

13. The Nicetes whom Philostratus counts as the first representative of the Second Sophistic may have been related to a speaker of the same name under Augustus; L. Radermacher, *RE* 17 (1936) 319–321.

14. For the geography, F. Bölte, *RE* 3 A (1929) 1312–14; C. A. Roebuck, *A History of Messenia from 369 to 146 B.C.* (Chicago, 1941) 118–121, with map, 128; E. Philippson and E. Kirsten, *Die griechischen Landschaften* 3.2 (Frankfurt, 1959) 423; G. Steinhauer, *Ariadne* 4 (1988) 219–233 *(non vidi)*. For the present discussion, it does not much matter that the precise location is uncertain.

15. In general, Tac. *Ann.* 4.43; for the inscription from Olympia setting out the Milesian decision, *Syll.*[3] 683 = Curty, *Parentés* 6.

16. Tac. *Ann.* 4.43.2. "Rocks" presumably refers to boundary mark-

ings, such as actually survive (*IG* 5.1, 1371–72); "bronze," to records in temples.

17. For a decision in the matter taken by a freedman of Vespasian, *IG* 5.1, 1431; Roebuck, *Messenia* 14 n. 37.

18. Tac. *Ann.* 4.43.2.

19. In general, M. Sartre, *L'Orient romain* 211–219; S. E. Alcock, *Graecia Capta* (Cambridge, 1993), arguing that some of the apparent "decline" was due to changes in settlement patterns.

20. The classic study is G. W. Bowersock, *Greek Sophists in the Roman Empire* (Oxford, 1969); a good summary by E. L. Bowie in *OCD*[3] s.v. "Second Sophistic"; see now T. Schmitz, *Bildung und Macht: Zur sozialen und politischen Funktion der zweiten Sophistik* (Munich, 1997).

21. Plut. *Praec. ger. reip.* 808 B, 816 C.

22. In general, W. Ruge, *RE* 4 A (1931) 322–325; G. E. Bean in *PECS* 861; for the inscriptions, M. Ç. Sahin, *IStratonikeia*.

23. J. Schaefer, *De Iove apud Cares culto* 417–418; A. Laumonier, *Les cultes indigènes en Carie* 241–242; *IStratonikeia* 266.

24. J. Hatzfeld, *BCH* 51 (1927) 71–78 = *SEG* 4.247–261; *IStratonikeia* 22–39; Curty, *Parentés* 70.

25. *IStratonikeia* 22 = Curty, *Parentés* 70a.

26. *IStratonikeia* 25.4, 27.6, etc.

27. Carians in islands: Hdt. 1.171.2, Thuc. 1.8.1. Miletus: Homer *Il.* 2.868; cf. Hdt. 1.142.3.

28. *TAM* II 174, esp. Da 7–12; *FGrH* 770 F 5; A. Chaniotis, *Historie und Historiker in den griechischen Inschriften* 75–85; Curty, *Parentés* 79.

29. *TAM* II 174 C 16–D 2. See Appendix 2.

30. L. Robert, *OMS* VII 225–282, esp. 265–266 on the city's Macedonian origins.

31. For a list of cities which display Perseus on their coins, L. Robert, *Documents d'Asie Mineure* 74–77.

32. Robert, *Documents* 77–86; Curty, *Parentés* 5.

33. Assuming that the word "Asia" is correctly restored in line 24: see the apparatus in Curty, *Parentés*.

34. A good overview, though limited in time, is R. Pera, *Homonoia sulle monete da Augusto agli Antonini* (Genoa, 1984); also U.

Kampmann, *Die Homonoia-Verträge der Stadt Pergamon* (Saarbrücken, 1996).

35. H. von Aulock, *Jb. f. Numism. u. Geldgesch.* 19 (1969) 85–86; Pera, *Homonoia* 58–61; Kampmann, *Homonoia* 59–74. Wealthy Pergamene: *IG* 12.2.243, with the discussion of L. Robert, *OMS* VII 576–577; Curty, *Parentés* 22.

36. *OGIS* 536.

37. Philostr. *Vit. Soph.* 1.24.3, 41–42 Kayser.

38. On the different senses of *mētropolis,* and its appearance in the civic titulature of this period, G. W. Bowersock, *Bonner Historia-Augusta Colloquium 1982–1983* 75–88.

39. P. Herrmann, *Chiron* 23 (1993) 238–243.

40. On these expressions and their significance, see esp. L. Robert, *OMS* VI 228.

41. *OGIS* 603; on the city's relations with Rome, E. Honigmann, *RE* 12 (1924) 714–715.

42. Sartre, *L'Orient romain* 195–196.

43. On this, A. S. Spawforth and S. M. Walker, *JRS* 75 (1985) 78–104, 76 (1986) 88–105; C. P. Jones, *Chiron* 26 (1996) 29–56.

44. *OGIS* 503, with Dittenberger's excellent commentary; J. H. Oliver, *Marcus Aurelius* (Princeton, 1970) 5. Cf. the very similar inscription set up by the city of Cibyra in the Italian port of Puteoli, *OGIS* 497 = Oliver, *Marcus Aurelius* 6; on this see now S. Follet, *Bull. épigr.* 1996 195.

45. *IG* 5.1.452; see now Jones, *Chiron* 26 (1996) 39–41, 51–56.

46. In general, Habicht, *Ist. Mitt.* 9/10 (1959–1960) 110–127; Habicht, *IPergamon (Asklepieion)* 8, 141; O. Andrei, *A. Claudius Charax di Pergamo* (Bologna, 1984). For the fragments, Jacoby, *FGrH* 103. Epigram: Suda s.v. Charax = *FGrH* 103 T 1.

47. Nestor and Pisander: L. Robert, *OMS* VII 588 n. 71; P. Weiss, *Chiron* 20 (1990) 228–234; J. D. Denniston, S. Hornblower, and A. J. S. Spawforth, *OCD*[3] 1390 (Septimius Nestor). Pisander's poem: Macrob. *Sat.* 5.2.4–5. Myth and coin: Weiss 235–237.

48. For the coins in question, N. Baydur, *Jb. f. Numism. u. Geldgesch.* 56 (1976) 56, nos. 366–368, with the discussion of P. Weiss, *Chiron* 21 (1991) 373 n. 80.

10. Late Antiquity

1. In general, P. Brown, *The Making of Late Antiquity* (Cambridge, Mass., 1978); G. W. Bowersock, *Hellenism in Late Antiquity* (Ann Arbor, 1990); for one case study, C. Roueché, *Aphrodisias in Late Antiquity*. Hdt. 8.144.2.

2. N. Wilson, ed., *Saint Basil: On the Value of Greek Literature* (London, 1975).

3. L. Robert, *Hellenica* 4 (1948) 18 (but taking Θέμιδι as a personification); on the honorand, *PLRE* II 631–633, Isidorus 9.

4. Chor. Gaz. *Or.* 7 *(Or. fun. in Proc.)*; cf. Phot. *Bibl.* 102 B, with the comments of W. Schmid, *RE* 3 (1899) 2426–27. T. D. Barnes, however, considers Choricius a pagan; W. J. Slater, ed., *Roman Theater and Society* (Ann Arbor, 1996) 179–180.

5. D. A. Russell and N. G. Wilson, eds., *Menander Rhetor* (Oxford, 1981) 181–193. For the evolution of πρεσβεία, Stephanus (Hase) *Thes. Gr. Ling.* and G. W. H. Lampe, *Patristic Greek Lexicon* s.v.

6. Roueché, *Aphrodisias* 32; cf. C. P. Jones, *Hermes* 125 (1997) 212–214.

7. *Pan. Lat.* 5 (8). On the date and background, see now Nixon in C. E. V. Nixon and B. S. Rodgers, *In Praise of Later Roman Emperors* (Berkeley, 1994) 255–256.

8. *Pan. Lat.* 5 (8) 2.4.

9. *Pan. Lat.* 5 (8) 3.1–3, with Nixon's commentary; cf. above, Chapter 7.

10. On Themistius, see esp. G. Dagron, *Travaux et Mémoires* 3 (1968) 1–242; J. Vanderspoel, *Themistius and the Imperial Court.*

11. Them. *Or.* 4; Vanderspoel, *Themistius* 96–97.

12. Them. *Or.* 4, 53 A (temple), 55 A–B (senate and Constantius), 56 C (Vetranio).

13. Vanderspoel, *Themistius* 101–102; Amm. Marc. 16.10.4–17.

14. Them. *Or.* 3, 42 B (Rome as mother city), 47 E (Constantius and Romulus), 44 B (Magnentius), 47 D (Constantinople the sister of Constantius).

15. Vanderspoel, *Themistius* 61–65.

16. Lib. *Or.* 15. On this speech and its circumstances, G. W.

Bowersock, *Julian the Apostate* (Cambridge, Mass., 1978) 94–105; H.-U. Wiemer, *Libanios und Julian* (Munich, 1995) 217–227.

17. *Or.* 15.7; cf. Cic. *II Verr.* 2.4.81: "cognatio studiorum et artium propemodum non minus est coniuncta quam ista qua uos delectamini generis et nominis."

18. *Or.* 15.51. For Celsus, *PLRE* I 193–194, Celsus 3.

19. Lib. *Or.* 11. For this aspect of this much-discussed work, note especially A. D. Nock, *JEA* 40 (1954) 76–82.

20. *Or.* 11.42–130.

21. On the gate and its inscription, L. Robert, *Hellenica* 13 (1965) 158–163; Roueché, *Aphrodisias* 37–38, proposing Julian as the emperor whose name is erased (Curty, *Parentés* 74, overlooks Roueché). On the honorand, *PLRE* I 283 (Eros 2), 608 (Monaxius). As of July 1996 the block carrying the inscription lay near the Tetrapylon.

22. Lib. *Ep.* 94 Wolf. Thus *PLRE* and Roueché (previous note). In R. Förster's edition (X 96) this letter is attached to the preceding one.

23. Christians: e.g., C. Habicht in V. Milojčić and D. Theocharis, eds., *Demetrias* I (Bonn, 1976) 199–203 (a Christian girl descended from "Aiacides" or Achilles). Bishops such as "Aletodorus" at Corcyra, "Letodorus" at Cibyra: L. Robert, *Etudes épigraphiques et philologiques* (Paris, 1938) 211–212.

24. For Minos on the tomb of Zoilus, Chapter 8.

25. On this monument, Appendix 1 and Figure 4. I am very grateful to Bert Smith for discussion in July 1996.

26. A. Cameron, *Claudian* (Oxford, 1970) 11; G. Dagron, *Constantinople imaginaire* (Paris, 1984) 9–19; A. Berger, *Untersuchungen zu den Patria Konstantinupoleos* (Bonn, 1988) 35–37.

27. P. Chuvin, *Mythologie et géographie dionysiaques* 24–26 (Byzas), 179–180 (Perseus), 197–198 (Tyre and Beirut).

28. Nonnus *Dion.* 3.364–371; Chuvin, *Mythologie* 24–25.

29. On the date of Stephanus, E. Honigmann, *RE* 3 A (1929) 2369–74; on his purpose, H. Hunger, *Die hochsprachliche profane Literatur der Byzantiner* I (Munich, 1978) 530–531.

30. Justin. *Nov.* 25 praef.; cf. P. Weiss, *Chiron* 20 (1990) 223–225;

and, for Justinian's reform, *LRE* I 280. On the recipient, J. B. Bury, *History of the Later Roman Empire* II (London, 1923) 36–39, 55–61; *PLRE* III 627–635.

Conclusion

1. Hdt. 5.49 (Spartans), 5.97 (Athenians).
2. D. M. Lewis, *Sparta and Persia* (Leyden, 1977) 13–14; cf. Hdt. 1.135.1 on the Greeks in Cyrus' retinue.
3. Hdt. 7.151.
4. Plut. *Ant.* 36.6. Cf. Philip V's famous declaration on the Roman practice of granting citizenship to liberated slaves, *Syll.*³ 543.32–34, with the comments of P. Gauthier in *Mélanges d'histoire ancienne offerts à William Seston* (Paris, 1974) 207–215.
5. For some of these differences of language and form, J. Linderski in E. Frézouls and A. Jacquemin, eds., *Les relations internationales* (Paris, 1995) 453–78.
6. Isocr. *Paneg.* 50. Cf. F. W. Walbank, *Selected Papers* (1985) 1–19.
7. Aristid. *Or.* 26.63.
8. On revocation of the *civitas,* T. Mommsen, *Römisches Strafrecht* (Leipzig, 1899) 956–959.
9. Cleanth. *Hymn.* 4; Arat. *Phaen.* 5; Ap. Tyan. *Ep.* 44.2, with the commentary of R. J. Penella. In general, E. Des Places, *Syngeneia* 137–141.
10. *Act. Ap.* 17.28, citing Arat. *Phaen.* 5.
11. Christian language: Luc. *Peregr.* 13; *Passio Pionii* 18.7, with the commentary of L. Robert. For *synteknia,* C. Rapp, *Traditio* 52 (1997) 293–296, 302–304.

Appendix 1

1. J. Bousquet, *REG* 101 (1988) 12–53; *SEG* 38.1476; Curty, *Parentés* 75. See now C. D. Hadzis, *BCH* 121 (1997) 1–14.
2. *SEG* 38.1476.24–30.
3. Bousquet, *REG* 101 (1988) 35.
4. LSJ s.v. ἀποικίζω, "*send away from home* . . . Pass., *to be settled in a far land.*"
5. Xen. *Oec.* 7.34, trans. S. Pomeroy.
6. Hdt. 1.94.

7. LSJ s.v. πολεμόω: "Pass., also in early writers, *have war made upon one, be treated as enemies*"; LSJ s.v. ὁρμάω B 2 b, "in historical prose, ὁρμᾶσθαι ἐκ, *start from, begin from*, of a general, *making that place his head-quarters or base of operation*."

8. J. Toepffer, *RE* 1 (1893) 1369–71.

9. Paus. 2.4.3.

10. L. Robert, *Hellenica* 5 (1948) 5–15; a revised text in N. F. Jones, *TAPA* 110 (1980) 165–166, whence *SEG* 30.990; L. Robert, *Hellenica* 11/12 (1960) 562–569, esp. 568 n. 3; Jones 165–172; in disagreement, G. R. Stanton, *Classical Antiquity* 5 (1986) 139–153 = *SEG* 36.308. On the family of Pausimachus, C. Habicht, *Hesperia* 60 (1991) 210–211. Aletes and tribes of Corinth: *Suda* p; 225 Adler; cf. Jones 162, 187.

11. Paus. 2.4.3 (Ornytion); cf. 10.4.10, tomb of a *heros archēgetēs,* identified by some with Phocus, by others with Xanthippus, the Phocian general of the third century, on whom see *Syll.*³ 361 (*FD* 3.4.218–222). On Phocus, N. Icard-Gianolio, *LIMC* 7.1 (1994) 396; on the location of this tomb, see now J. McInerney, *Hesperia* 66 (1997) 193–207.

12. St. Byz. 461.15 Meineke.

13. St. Byz. 287.16; cf. 287.5 on "Euromus," in fact an alternative spelling of the same name: L. Robert, *Hellenica* 8 (1950) 35–37.

14. St. Byz. 696.9–14 = *FGrH* 740 F 8; the phrase "and the Chrysaorians" was added by Meineke, and is surely necessary.

15. A new inscription shows their *syngeneia* with the obscure Angeira of Pisidia: J. Bousquet and P. Gauthier, *REG* 106 (1993) 12–23, esp. 19 n. 8.

16. Coins: D. J. MacDonald, *The Coinage of Aphrodisias* (London, 1992) 108 Type 126 with plate XV. Names "Chrysaor," etc.: *CIG* 2821, 2847, on which J. and L. Robert, *Fouilles d'Amyzon en Carie* (1983) 224 n. 19 ("il ne s'agit là que d'un souvenir historique"). Statue-base and relief: R. R. R. Smith in *Aphrodisias Papers* 3 (1996) 56. Ninos Frieze: Pl. 4.

17. For the system of *sympoliteiai* in Asia, L. Robert, *Villes d'Asie Mineure*² (Paris, 1962) 54–64, 272; J. Bousquet and P. Gauthier, *REG* 107 (1994) 328–330. On Bingeç, R. R. R. Smith and C. Ratté, *AJA* 99 (1995) 40–41.

18. For a Tauropolis somewhere between Caria and Lycia, B. Kruse, *RE* 5 A (1936) 33, "Tauropoleites"; W. Ruge, ibid. 33–34, "Tauropolis 3" (these two articles apparently written in ignorance of each other).

Appendix 2

1. *TAM* II 174; *FGrH* 770 F 5; Curty, *Parentés* 79; above, Chapter 9.
2. *TAM* II 174 B 1–2.
3. Hdt. 1.171.6.
4. H. J. Mette, *RE* 21 (1952) 1596 no. 6; Jacoby, *FGrH* 770.
5. On Panyassis, F. Stoessl, *RE* 18.2 (1949) 871–923; V. J. Matthews, *Panyassis of Halikarnassos* (Leyden, 1974); for the fragments, Bernabé, *Poet. Epic. Gr.* I 171–181. On this fragment, 23 Bernabé, see esp. G. R. Huxley, *GRBS* 5 (1964) 29–33.
6. There is no article in *RE* on the river, though an excellent one on the city, P. Demargne and H. Metzger, *RE* 9 A (1967) 1375–1408.
7. Strabo 14.3.6, 665 C, ὁ Ξάνθος ποταμός, ἵν Σίρβιν ἐκάλουν τὸ πρότερον; Eust. *Il.* III 400, 23 van der Valk (Σίρμις). Cf. J. Tischler, *Kleinasiatische Hydronomie* (Wiesbaden, 1977) 136–137.
8. Lycian Xanthus in Homer: *Il.* 2.877, 6.172. Xanthus in the Troad: *Il.* 21.8.
9. T. A. B. Spratt and E. Forbes, *Travels in Lycia, Milyas, and the Cibyratis, in company with the late Rev. E. T. Daniell* (London, 1847) vii (purpose of visit), 12 (the Xanthus), 38–39 (visit to the source near the village of "Orahn").
10. *SEG* 28.1245, B 6. The relevance of the inscription to Panyassis is noticed by P. Frei in J. Borchhardt and G. Dobesch, eds., *Akten des II. Internationalen Lykien-Symposions* I (Vienna, 1993) 88 n. 15.
11. On the mountain range and the city of this name, W. Ruge, *RE* 11 (1922) 1567, "Kragos" 1 and 2.
12. Hdt. 1.173.1–3.
13. Apollod. *Bibl.* 3.1.2. I am grateful to Hugh Lloyd-Jones for advice on this point.
14. J. Zahle in O. Mørkholm and J. Zahle, *Acta Archaeologica* 43 (1972) 101.
15. Zahle in Mørkholm and Zahle, *Acta Archaeologica* 47 (1976) 86; here, Figure 5 = *BMC Lycia* 30 no. 132, reverse.

SELECT BIBLIOGRAPHY

Alty, J. H. M. "Dorians and Ionians." *JHS* 102 (1982) 1–14.

Asheri, D. *Fra Ellenismo e Iranismo: Studi sulla Società e Cultura di Xanthos nella Età achemenide.* Bologna, 1983.

Bickermann, E. J. "Origines Gentium." *CP* 47 (1952) 65–81 = *Religion and Politics in the Hellenistic and Roman Periods* (1985) 399–417.

Bickermann, E. J., and J. Sykutris. *Speusipps Brief an König Philipp.* Berichte über die Verhandlungen der Sächischen Akademie der Wissenschaften zu Leipzig, Philol.-hist. Kl. 80, 3. Leipzig, 1928.

Bousquet, J. "La stèle des Kyténiens au Létôon de Xanthos." *REG* 101 (1988) 12–53.

Bowersock, G. W. "Hadrian and Metropolis." In *Bonner Historia-Augusta Colloquium 1982–1983* (Bonn, 1985) 75–88 = *Studies on the Eastern Roman Empire* (Goldbach bei Aschaffenburg, 1994) 371–384.

Bravo, B. "Sulân. Représailles et justice privée contre des étrangers dans les cités grecques." *Annali della Scuola Normale Superiore di Pisa,* 3d ser., 10 (1980) 675–987.

Chamoux, F. *Cyrène sous la monarchie des Battiades.* BEFAR 177. Paris, 1952.

Chaniotis, A. *Historie und Historiker in den griechischen Inschriften: Epigraphische Beiträge zur griechischen Historiographie*. Stuttgart, 1988.

Chuvin, P. *Mythologie et géographie dionysiaques: Recherches sur l'oeuvre de Nonnos de Panopolis*. Clermont-Ferrand, 1992.

Curty, O. "A propos de la parenté entre Juifs et Spartiates." *Historia* 41 (1992) 246–248.

———— "A propos de la συγγένεια entre cités." *REG* 107 (1994) 698–707.

———— "La notion de la parenté entre cités chez Thucydide." *Museum Helveticum* 51 (1994) 193–197.

———— *Les parentés légendaires entre cités grecques*. Geneva, 1995.

Dench, E. *From Barbarians to New Men: Greek, Roman, and Modern Perceptions of Peoples of the Central Apennines*. Oxford, 1995.

Derow, P. S. "Pharos and Rome." *ZPE* 88 (1991) 261–270.

Des Places, E. *Syngeneia: La parenté de l'homme avec dieu, d'Homère à la patristique*. Paris, 1964.

Ebert, J. "Zur Stiftungsurkunde der ΛΕΥΚΟΦΡΥΗΝΑ in Magnesia am Mäander (Inschr. v. Magn. 16)." *Philologus* 126 (1982) 198–216.

Elwyn, S. "Interstate Kinship and Roman Foreign Policy." *TAPA* 123 (1993) 261–286.

Erim, K. T. *Aphrodisias: City of Venus Aphrodite*. Oxford, 1986.

Ferrary, J.-L. *Philhellénisme et impérialisme: Aspects idéologiques de la conquête romaine du monde hellénistique*. BEFAR 271. Rome, 1988.

Gauthier, P. "Les saisies licites aux dépens des étrangers dans les cités grecques." *Revue historique des droits français et étranger* 60 (1982) 553–576.

Gomme, A. W., A. Andrewes, and K. J. Dover. *A Historical Commentary on Thucydides*. 5 vols. Oxford, 1945–1981.

Gruen, E. S. *Culture and National Identity in Republican Rome*. Ithaca, 1992.

———— *The Hellenistic World and the Coming of Rome*. Berkeley, 1984.

———— "The Jewish-Spartan Affiliation." In *Transitions to Empire: Essays in Greco-Roman History 360–146 B.C. in Honor of E. Badian*. Norman, Okla. 1996. Pp. 254–270.

Habicht, C. *Athens from Alexander to Antony.* Cambridge, Mass., 1997.

Hall, E., *Inventing the Barbarian: Greek Self-Definition through Tragedy.* Oxford, 1989.

Hall, J. M. *Ethnic Identity in Greek Antiquity.* Cambridge, 1997.

Hammond, N. G. L., G. T. Griffith, and F. W. Walbank. *A History of Macedonia.* 3 vols. Oxford, 1972–1988.

Hornblower, S. *A Commentary on Thucydides.* 2 vols. to date. Oxford, 1991–.

——— "The Religious Dimension to the Peloponnesian War, Or, What Thucydides Does Not Tell Us." *HSCP* 94 (1992) 169–196.

Hornblower, S., and A. J. S. Spawforth, eds. *The Oxford Classical Dictionary,* 3d ed. Oxford, 1996.

Jones, C. P. *"Graia pandetur ab urbe." HSCP* 97 (1995) 233–241.

——— "The Panhellenion." *Chiron* 26 (1996) 29–56.

——— "Vergil and the Lycians." In *Studies for Dante: Essays in Honor of Dante della Terza,* ed. F. Fido, R. A. Syska-Lamparska, and P. D. Stewart (Fiesole, 1998). Pp. 19–23.

Jones, C. P., and J. Russell. "Two New Inscriptions from Nagidos in Cilicia." *Phoenix* 47 (1993) 293–304.

Jones, N. F. "The Civic Organization of Corinth." *TAPA* 110 (1980) 161–193.

Kienast D. "Presbeia." *RE* Suppl. 13 (1973) 499–628.

——— "Rom und die Venus vom Eryx." *Hermes* 93 (1965) 478–489.

Laumonier, A. *Les cultes indigènes en Carie.* BEFAR 188. Paris, 1958.

Lévêque, P. *Pyrrhos.* BEFAR 185. Paris, 1957.

Lexicon iconographicum Mythologiae classicae (LIMC). 8 vols. to date. Zurich, 1981–.

Lomas, K. *Rome and the Western Greeks 350 B.C.–A.D. 200: Conquest and Acculturation in Southern Italy.* London, 1993.

Malkin, I. *Religion and Colonization in Ancient Greece.* Studies in Greek and Roman Religion 3. Leiden, 1987.

McGing, B. C. *The Foreign Policy of Mithridates VI Eupator. Mnemosyne* Suppl. 89. Leiden, 1986.

Meadows, A. "Four Rhodian Decrees: Rhodes, Iasos and Philip V." *Chiron* 26 (1996) 251–265.

Momigliano, A. D. *Alien Wisdom: The Limits of Hellenization.* London, 1975.

Musti, D. "Sull' idea di συγγένεια in iscrizioni greche." *Annali della Scuola Normale Superiore di Pisa,* 2d ser., 32 (1963) 225–239.

Nicolson, H. G. *Diplomacy.* 2d ed. London, 1950.

Nilsson, M. P. *Cults, Myths, Oracles, and Politics in Ancient Greece.* Lund, 1951.

Nock, A. D. "The Praises of Antioch." *Journ. Eg. Arch.* 40 (1954) 76–82.

Reynolds, J. M. *Aphrodisias and Rome. Journal of Roman Studies* Monographs 1. London, 1982.

Rigsby, K. J. *Asylia: Territorial Inviolability in the Hellenistic world.* Berkeley, 1996.

Robert, J., and L. Robert. *La Carie* 2: *Le plateau de Tabai et ses environs.* Paris, 1954.

——— *Fouilles d'Amyzon en Carie* 1. Paris, 1983.

Robert, L. *A travers l'Asie Mineure: Poètes et prosateurs, monnaies grecques, voyageurs et géographie.* BEFAR 239. Paris, 1980.

——— "De Cilicie à Messine et à Plymouth avec deux inscriptions grecques errantes." *Journal des savants* 1975 161–211 = *OMS* VII 225–275.

——— "Un décret dorien trouvé à Délos." *Hellenica* 5 (1948) 5–15.

——— "Deux poètes grecs à l'époque impériale." in *Stele: Tomos eis Mnemen Nikolaou Kontoleontos.* Athens, 1980. Pp. 1–20 = *OMS* VII 569–588.

——— *Documents d'Asie Mineure.* BEFAR 239 bis. Paris 1987.

——— *Etudes anatoliennes.* Paris, 1937.

——— "Héraclès à Pergame et une épigramme de l'Anthologie XVI 91." *Rev. Phil.* 58 (1984) 7–18 = *OMS* VI 457–468.

——— "Les juges étrangers dans la cité grecque." In *Xenion. Festschrift für Pan. I. Zepos.* Athens, 1973. Pp. 765–782 = *OMS* V 137–154.

——— *Monnaies antiques en Troade.* Geneva, 1966.

——— "Nonnos et les monnaies d'Akmonia de Phrygie." *Journal des savants* 1975 153–192 = *OMS* VII 185–224.

———— "Notes d'épigraphie hellénistique XXVIII: Inscription d'Istros." *BCH* 52 (1928) 170–172 = *OMS* I 99–101.

———— "Pergame d'Epire." *Hellenica* 1 (1940) 95–105.

———— "Les théores de Pergame." *REG* 40 (1927) 208–213 = *OMS* I 449–454.

Roueché, C. *Aphrodisias in Late Antiquity. Journal of Roman Studies* Monographs 5. London, 1989.

Sartre, M. *L'Orient romain: Provinces et sociétés provinciales en Méditerranée orientale d'Auguste aux Sévères (31 avant J.-C.–235 après J.-C.).* Paris, 1991.

Schaefer, J. *De Iove apud Cares culto.* Halle, 1912.

Scheer, T. S. *Mythische Vorväter: Zur Bedeutung griechischer Heroenmythen im Selbstverständnis kleinasiatischer Städte.* Munich, 1993.

Schilling, R. *La religion romaine de Vénus, depuis les origines jusqu'au temps d'Auguste.* BEFAR 178. Paris, 1954.

Schlesinger, E. *Die griechische Asylie.* Giessen, 1933.

Schürer, E. *The History of the Jewish People in the Age of Jesus Christ.* Rev. ed. Ed. E. Vermes, F. Millar, and M. Goodman. 3 vols. in 4. Edinburgh, 1973–1987.

Spawforth, A. S., and S. M. Walker. "The World of the Panhellenion I. Athens and Eleusis." *JRS* 75 (1985) 78–104.

———— "The World of the Panhellenion II. Three Dorian Cities." *JRS* 76 (1986) 88–105.

Stern, M. *Greek and Roman Authors on Jews and Judaism.* 3 vols. Jerusalem, 1974–1984.

Strubbe, J. H. M. "Gründer kleinasiatischer Städte: Fiktion und Realität." *Ancient Society* 15–17 (1984–1986) 253–304.

Vanderspoel, J. *Themistius and the Imperial Court: Oratory, Civic Duty, and Paideia from Constantius to Theodosius.* Ann Arbor, 1995.

Walbank, F. W. *A Historical Commentary on Polybius.* 3 vols. Oxford, 1957–1979.

———— "The Problem of Greek Nationality." *Phoenix* 5 (1951) 41–60 = *Selected Papers: Studies in Greek and Roman History and Historiography.* Cambridge, 1985. Pp. 1–19.

Weiss, P. "Auxe Perge: Beobachtungen zu einem bemerkenswerten städtischen Document des späten 3. Jahrhunderts n. Chr." *Chiron* 21 (1991) 353–392.

————— "Mythen, Dichter und Münzen von Lykaonien." *Chiron* 20 (1990) 221–237.

West, M. L. *The Hesiodic Catalogue of Women*. Oxford, 1985.

Will, E. *Histoire politique du monde hellénistique*. 2d ed. 2 vols. Nancy, 1979–1982.

————— "Syngeneia, Oikeiotès, Philia." *Rev. Phil.* 69 (1995) 299–325.

INDEX

REVEALING ANTIQUITY

G. W. Bowersock, General Editor